Nice, Cannes & Monte Carlo

Front cover: Monte Carlo and the ...

Below: The preferred means of transport in Monte Carlo

Jardin Exotique • Monaco's cliffside fantasy land of cactuses *(page 75)*

Musée Matisse • Nice is home to this unmissable collection from all stages of the artist's career *(page 48)*

Promenade des Anglais • The legendary footpath epitomises the elegance of Belle Epoque Nice and is lined with glorious beaches and iconic hotels *(page 38)*

La Croisette • Cannes's animated seafront promenade is a must for watching the world go by *(page 51)*

Colline du Château Nothing remains of the medieval citadel, but glorious views of Nice abound *(page 31)*

Casino de Monte Carlo Opened in 1863, the Casino is still the ultimate symbol of Monaco glamour *(page 63)*

Marché Forville Cannes's colourful feast of wonderful Riviera produce *(page 54)*

Vieux Nice An atmospheric Italianate maze of narrow streets and coloured campaniles *(page 26)*

Cathédrale Orthodoxe Russe Saint-Nicolas A touch of Russian flamboyance on the Riviera *(page 44)*

Iles de Lérins Escape the Cannes crowds and make the quick boat trip to these charming islands *(page 58)*

CONTENTS

Introduction 7

A Brief History 13

Where to Go 25

A ➤ in the text denotes a highly recommended sight

Nice 25

Vieux Nice 25, Cours Saleya 27, The Colline du Château 31, The Vieux Port 32, Promenade du Paillon 34, Promenades des Arts 35, The New Town 37, Promenade des Anglais 38, Western Nice 42, Parc Floral Phoenix 43, North of the Station 44, Cimiez 46

Cannes 50

La Croisette 51, The Port Vieux and Marché Forville 53, Le Suquet 55, La Croix des Gardes 56, Le Cannet 57, La Californie 58, The Iles de Lérins 58, Ile Sainte-Marguerite 59, Ile Saint-Honorat 61

Monaco 62

Monte Carlo 63, Around the Casino 65, Further East 66, La Condamine 67, Monaco-Ville 69, Exploring the Old Town 70, Cathedral and Aquarium 71, Fontvieille 73, A Trio of Museums 74, Moneghetti 75

Excursions 76

Cagnes-sur-Mer 76, The Musée Renoir 77, Mougins 78, The Estérel 79

55

72

42

What to Do............................ 83

Shopping............................. 83

Arts and Entertainment 86

Nightlife 89

Sports and Activities...................... 91

Children 94

Eating Out........................ 97

Handy Travel Tips.............. 106

Hotels and Restaurants....... 127

Index.............................. 143

12

99

62

Features

On Track for Art 11

Ludovico Bréa 16

Historical Landmarks 23

The Ecole de Nice 36

Beaches for All 39

Cannes Film Festival 52

Monaco Grand Prix 66

Matisse's Chapel 76

Venturing Inland 81

Carnaval de Nice 86

Calendar of Events 96

Portable Treats 98

INTRODUCTION

Nice, Cannes, Monaco. The three names alone evoke many of the myths of the Côte d'Azur, each endowed with grandiose architecture and spectacular natural settings: the Baie de Cannes with the backdrop of the red Estérel mountains to the west, Nissa la Bella (Beautiful Nice) sitting on the glorious curve of the Baie des Anges, or the crazy piled-up tower blocks of Monaco, clustered between sea and the white limestone crags of the Alpine foothills.

The gentle Mediterranean climate made the French Riviera a magnet for the aristocratic winter visitors of the Belle Epoque, and its quality of light attracted Matisse, Picasso, Bonnard, de Staël and countless other artists during the 20th century. Today, mild sunny winters interspersed by just a few chilly days, crisp spring sunlight and the guarantee of hot summers with a sea that's like bathing in bathwater continue to draw tourists from the world over.

Yet unlike some southern French resorts, which are deserted in the off season, these are active year-round cities. Nice is the administrative capital of the Alpes-Maritimes *département*, with a dynamic cultural scene, a growing university, a large services sector and a nearby hi-tech science park at Sophia Antipolis. Cannes glories in film-star kudos yet resounds to a busy congress schedule that is fuelled by a non-stop succession of TV producers, music industry magnates, property developers and experts in all things luxurious (the luxury shopping, tourism and yachting industries all descend here for their trade fairs). Monaco's casinos now merely play a supporting role to the profits generated by luxury spas and financial and banking services.

The dome of the Negresco, Nice's most famous hotel

Architectural Heritage

All three cities have an architectural heritage begging to be discovered. The late 16th- and 17th-century expansion of Nice below Castle Hill gave Vieux Nice pretty much the Italianate Baroque face it still has today, with pastel-coloured campaniles, imposing Genoese-style palaces, such as Palais Lascaris, and richly decorated churches, like the Cathédrale Sainte-Réparate, the Gésu and the Miséricorde and Sainte-Rita chapels, where relatively sober facades hide interiors awash with the carving, stucco and fake marble, sculpted saints and cherubs, sunbursts and barleysugar columns that marked the Catholic Counter-Reformation.

Sunset over Monaco's high-rise architecture

Above all, the late 19th and early 20th centuries shaped the architectural flavour of the cities, when the Riviera developed as a chic winter destination for the European aristocracy. The Belle Epoque was marked by eclectic decoration – neo-Gothic, neo-Renaissance, neoclassical and neo-Louis XIII were all utilised in banks, hotels, casinos, villas and churches. The winter gardens of the Negresco and Hermitage hotels and the Art Deco Palais de la Méditerranée in Nice give today's visitors a hint of what life was like, at least for the wealthy, in the cities' heyday.

Cities of Contrast

Perhaps part of the appeal of all three destinations and one of the reasons they continue to fascinate are their apparent paradoxes. Palatial seafront hotels contrast with the charm of narrow village streets; luxury yachts drop anchor alongside the few remaining *pointu* fishing boats; shop windows displaying diamond necklaces contrast with the stalls at daily food markets overflowing with local produce.

Monaco's residents

Of Monaco's 32,000 residents, just 7,000 are Monégasque citizens entitled to vote for the Conseil National. They are easily outnumbered by 10,000 French. It is rare for foreigners to be awarded citizenship: a recent exception, in 2008, was chef Alain Ducasse, whose cooking at the renowned Le Louis XV gave the principality its first Michelin three-starred restaurant.

Nice combines all the allure of an elegant seaside resort with the urban pulse of a working city. With a population of 350,000, it is France's fifth city and heart of a conurbation of nearly 900,000, with Roman remains, fine architecture, world-class art museums, wide-ranging shops and a vibrant culinary scene. Long the capital of the quasi-independent Comté de Nice, later a cosmopolitan winter destination, Nice offers the charm of the narrow *ruelles* of its Old Town and the elegance of the planned streets of the new. In Cannes, the *département*'s third city (after Nice and Antibes), with a population of 67,000, an undeniably snobby aspect of extortionately priced beaches and posey restaurants coexists with the more popular charm of its covered market, the Provençal village atmosphere of Le Suquet and the democracy of the evening stroll along La Croisette.

In Monaco the modernity of skyscraper architecture and daring land reclamation schemes (the principality has grown in area by 25 percent since World War II) contrasts with the

The Vieux Port at Cannes

seeming anachronism of one of the world's tiniest monarchies: ostensibly a constitutional monarchy since 1911, signs of royalty are everywhere in this highly autocratic state. The 7,000 Monégasque citizens may elect the Conseil National of 24 parliamentarians every five years, but real power rests with the Sovereign Prince, who signs all ordinances and nominates (subject to approval by France) the Minister of State and five other members of government.

Image Makeover

Not everything is rosy when everyone wants to live in the sun. Urban sprawl has disfigured much of the coast. Pressure for land and flats bought by often absent tax exiles makes Monaco far too expensive for most of its employees to live there. There's a shortage of housing, too, in Cannes, where people prefer to let flats at high prices to festival-goers, congress clientele and tourists than to the local population; while the contrasts between rich and poor are striking in Nice's housing estates and the villas of Mont Boron.

But Nice is undergoing a renaissance. After a period at the end of the 20th century when it was stricken by its reputation for financial corruption, prostitution rings, an association with far right politics and an image as the dowager of the Riviera, Nice has emerged in a refreshed mood, the population rejuvenated by a growing number of students and the international set who have colonised Vieux Nice. Stimulated by low-cost flights from all over the world and the end of the Eastern Bloc, Nice once again has the sort of cosmopolitan feel it had in the Belle Epoque, even if it is no longer the playground of the aristocracy. The urban fabric, too, is experiencing a renewal: streets have been cleaned, buildings are being renovated and a new sense of civic pride was symbolised by the repaving of place Masséna for the opening of the pristine new tramway in 2007 *(see box below)*.

On Track for Art

In what Nice describes as 'the largest open-air museum in France', works commissioned from 15 international artists lining the length of the tramway have renewed the city's image as a creative centre. Several works – Jaume Plensa's translucent resin figures squatting atop poles in place Masséna, Yann Kersalé's blue lights criss-crossing avenue Jean Médecin, Gunda Förster's blue lines in homage to Klein along two railway bridges, and Ange Leccia's setting sun at Las Planas – are illuminated by night. Elsewhere, Pascal Pinaud and Stéphane Magnin reused elements from municipal lighting to create cheerfully chaotic new lamp-posts and Michael Craig Martin painted murals of everyday objects down the side of four housing blocks. The journey itself becomes an art experience, too, with station signs in curly calligraphy by local artist Ben. There are guided visits to the tramway's artworks in English and French every Friday evening; reserve at the tourist office.

On the beach in Cannes

Monaco, too, is trying to change its image. Somerset Maugham, who owned a house at Saint-Jean-Cap-Ferrat, called the principality 'a sunny place for shady people', and after the ignominy of its being put on the OECD blacklist of tax havens, Prince Albert II has brought in a new team of councillors and vowed to make banking practices more transparent.

A Greener Future

Perhaps the element that most typifies the new century is environmental awareness. In Monaco, Albert II is trying to promote the principality's environmental image through his Foundation for the Environment and a marine reserve just beyond Larvotto Beach (a green approach that is not, however, easy to reconcile with a plan to build a 1km (½-mile) peninsula, jutting out to sea near the Grimaldi Forum, which could have adverse effects on the marine ecosystem). The new mayor of Nice, Christian Estrosi, elected in 2008, has plans for a second east–west tram route, which should take some of the traffic off the promenade des Anglais; and an ambitious 'Eco-Vallée' near the airport (France's second-busiest), set to include a new commercial port, congress centre and football stadium on the western edge of town. Cannes now has a wide-ranging charter for sustainable development, from protection of the natural spaces of the Iles de Lérins and La Croix des Gardes to stabilisation of the beaches, water conservation, energy-efficient street lighting, new cycle lanes and electric buses.

A BRIEF HISTORY

Although just a few kilometres apart, Nice, Cannes and Monaco have had contrasting histories, often poised on opposing sides: Cannes as part of Provence and, later, France; Nice long an independent city state linked to Genoa and the house of Savoy; and Monaco, a tiny autocratic principality.

Beginnings

During the 4th century BC, Phocaean Greeks from Massilia (Marseille) founded trading posts named Nikaia (probably after *nike* for victory), roughly on the site of what is now Vieux Nice, and Monoikos (Monaco). However, traces of human settlement go back much earlier, to Terra Amata at the foot of Mont Boron, where a tribe of elephant-hunters camped some 400,000 years ago. Nearby Lazaret Cave, thought to have been inhabited 170,000 years ago, is still being excavated.

Ruins of the Roman amphitheatre at Fréjus

In the 1st century BC, the Romans defeated the Vediantii tribe and took over its hill settlement, renaming it Cemenelum (now Cimiez), on the strategic Via Julia Augusta between Italy and

Spain, making it capital of Alpes Maritimae province in AD 69. Cemenelum reached its peak in the 3rd century. Traces of the city, with three bathing establishments and a huge amphitheatre, can be seen at the Cimiez archaeological site.

Christianity gradually spread along the coast, and in 410 a monastery was founded on the island of Lérina (now Ile Saint-Honorat), which acquired extensive influence and territory (including Cannes) on the mainland. With the fall of the Roman Empire in 476, the region was invaded first by Barbarians from the East, then Saracens from North Africa, but it was the Franks who triumphed, establishing the Carolingian Empire, which stretched from western Germany to northern Spain and Italy. When Charlemagne's empire was divided in 843, Provence, nominally controlled by the Holy Roman Empire, was in effect an independent principality.

The medieval Château Grimaldi in Cagnes-sur-Mer

Counts Versus Consulats

In 972 Guillaume the Liberator drove the Saracens from their stronghold at La Garde Freinet in the Maures, bringing new prosperity to Provence, although the coast continued to suffer from marauding pirates. Fiercely independent Nice opposed the more centralised rule of the Provençal count and in 1144 established a Consulat, a sort of mini-republic whereby the town was administered by four elected consuls.

Count Ramon Berenger V, ruling from Aix-en-Provence since 1215, was determined to unify Provence and get rid of the consulates. In 1229 he invaded Nice, which had put itself under Genoese protection, and installed officials to administer the town. The count married all his daughters to kings or future kings: Marguerite to Louis IX of France, Eléonore to Henry III of England, Sanchia to Richard, earl of Cornwall, and Béatrice of Provence to Charles of Anjou, who thus inherited the title count of Provence in 1246, soon adding the kingdom of Sicily and Naples as well.

Meanwhile, Genoa had taken possession of Monaco and begun building a fortress. With Genoa caught up in the wars between the Guelph (pro-pope) and Ghibelline (pro-German emperor) factions, many of its noble families took refuge in eastern Provence, among them assorted branches of the Grimaldi family. In 1297, François Grimaldi, disguised as a monk, seized power as self-styled Seigneur of Monaco, establishing a new ruling dynasty (although it took the title of principality only in 1641).

Early 13th-century Nice prospered with the growth of important monasteries, and the town began to spread below the castle hill between the River Paillon and the sea. When Jeanne, countess of Provence and queen of Naples, chose Louis of Anjou, brother of French king Charles V, as her heir, rather than her cousin Charles III of Duras, Provence was divided. In 1382, Jeanne was assassinated near Naples, leading to a six-year civil war between pro-Anjou Marseille and pro-Duras Nice. In 1388 Nice submitted to Savoyard protection rather than that of Anjou, under the Dédition of Nice. Henceforth, Nice's fortunes were associated with Italy and the Holy Roman Empire, while Cannes on the western side of the River Var remained part of Provence, and Monaco – generally – sided with the French. With its sovereign conveniently far away, Nice enjoyed a new independence and prosperity from trade (essentially agricultural produce) with Italy, and an influx of Italian settlers bringing a culture distinguished by art and architecture, but the relationship also meant 400 years of on-off conflict with France.

Italians also settled elsewhere on the Riviera, brought in by landlords to cultivate land abandoned since the Black Death; while in a late flourishing of Gothic style, an artistic school grew up in Nice around the Bréa family *(see box below)*.

Power struggles intensified after 1481 when Provence was absorbed into the French kingdom. In the early 16th century, Nice thwarted the ambitions of François I, who hoped that he, rather than Charles I of Spain (future Emperor Charles

Ludovico Bréa

Louis or Ludovico Bréa was the leading figure of an artistic school that flourished in the Comté de Nice during the late 15th and early 16th century. Born in Nice in around 1450 to a family of barrel-makers who lived in rue Barillerie, he was soon carrying out commissions for churches and religious confraternities across the region. His powerful paintings mix the emotion of late Provençal Gothic with the discovery of perspective of the Italian Renaissance. You can see altarpieces by him (as well as works by his family and followers, including Antoine Bréa, François Brea, Giovanni Balaisin and Giovanni Canevesio) in several churches in Nice, Monaco, the southern Alpine valleys and across the Italian border.

V) would be elected Holy Roman Emperor. In 1538 Pope Paul III initiated negotiations between the French king, who stayed in the fortress at Villeneuve-Loubet, and Emperor Charles V, who resided at Villefranche-sur-Mer. The Treaty of Nice brought short-lived peace, but in 1543 the allied troops of François I and Turkish Sultan Suleiman the Magnificent besieged the city. According to local legend, on 15 August washerwoman Catherine Ségurane grabbed

Good King René ruled from 1434–80

a Turkish standard and pushed back the invaders. Although the lower town was sacked, the castle hill held out until relieved by Charles V's forces. Ségurane has gone down in local memory as a symbol of Niçois courage and feisty independence – although it is not certain that she ever existed.

Wars and Revolution

The expansion of Nice accelerated in the 17th century, when Emmanuel Philibert I converted the hilltop town into a bastioned citadel, and forced the population to move below, endowing Vieux Nice with Italianate Baroque style, with richly decorated churches and imposing Genoese-style palaces.

France besieged Nice again in 1691 and in 1705 during the War of Spanish Succession, when Savoyard Nice sided with the Habsburgs against French claims to the Spanish throne; in 1706 the citadel was razed, on the orders of Louis XIV, and this time not rebuilt. With Savoyard rule re-established, in 1782–92 King Victor-Amédée III of Sardinia laid out a grandiose arcaded square, the Piazza Vittoria (now place Garibaldi), at the entrance to town on the new route from his capital Turin, and began digging the new Port Lympia.

With the peasantry and bourgeoisie submerged by taxes to finance wars, and poor harvests leading to bread shortages, the people of Provence were active participants in the French Revolution; many of the aristocracy fled across the Var to take refuge in Nice. In 1792, the revolutionary Armée du Midi invaded Nice and Monaco, which remained under French rule until 1814, when the Treaty of Paris returned Nice to Sardinia-Piedmont and restored the prince of Monaco to his throne.

Winter Visitors

The 18th century saw the beginning of winter visitors from northern Europe. Lord and Lady Cavendish stayed in Nice in 1731, followed by other British aristocrats, among them the Duke of York in 1764, and by novelist Tobias Smollett, who described the town and its people in his *Travels Through France and Italy* (1766), admiring the remains of Cemenelum, treating Nice's 'slovenly' maids, 'greedy' shopkeepers and 'lazy' artisans with characteristic condescension and advocating the benefits of sea air for the lungs. By the 1780s some 300 British visitors wintered in Nice, settling to the west of town in a district they dubbed Newborough. In 1822, Reverend Lewis Way opened a public subscription for building a new seafront footpath, actually an employment exercise after a harsh winter, soon called the chemin des Anglais (renamed promenade des Anglais in 1844).

In 1834 British Lord Chancellor Henry Brougham was forced to overnight in Cannes because an outbreak of cholera prevented him crossing the border. He liked it so much he stayed, buying a plot of land and building the Villa Eléonore (named after his daughter) with gardens down to the sea. Cannes was transformed from a fishing village into an aristocratic watering hole for the English, who built elegant villas, mainly on the western side of town in the Quartier de la Croix des Gardes – fresh air and fine views being more important than proximity to the sea. Hotels were built for visitors and a veritable property market developed: Sir Thomas Woolfield was known for building extravagant residences, then selling them on, while in 1864 his former gardener, John Taylor, founded an estate agency that still exists today.

Reunification and Regeneration

In return for Napoleon III's support against Austria in the unification of Italy, King Victor Emmanuel II agreed to hand back Savoie and the Comté de Nice, confirmed by a vast majority in a referendum in April 1860. The population of the

The Casino on the pier at Nice

city nearly tripled between 1861 and 1911, boosted by the arrival of the railway in 1864, with people drawn in by the booming economy of Second Empire France. The expansion of the New Town continued in the Quartier des Musiciens, Les Baumettes and Cimiez, where the visit of Queen Victoria confirmed Nice as a fashionable destination. English aristocrats were joined by pleasure-seeking Russians, who built fairytale villas and the Russian Orthodox cathedral.

A treaty in 1861 also confirmed the attachment of Menton and Roquebrune, which had broken off from Monaco in the 1848 revolution. In search of new revenue, Prince Charles III turned to gambling, awarding the concession to run the Casino (banned in both neighbouring France and Italy) to businessman François Blanc, founder of the Société des Bains de Mer de Monaco. Blanc soon added the Hôtel de Paris to accommodate the gamblers and called in Parisian architect Charles Garnier to design an opera, adjoining the Casino, giving rise to a whole new district, Monte Carlo.

In the early 20th century, grand hotels went up along the seafront promenade in Cannes, and from 1922 the Calais Méditerranée Express, better known as the Train Bleu, bought British visitors direct from Calais to the Côte d'Azur. Americans introduced the new pleasures of sunbathing and water-skiing, and in 1931 the summer season was born when the grand hotels of Juan-les-Pins and Cannes stayed open in summer for the first time.

Avant-garde artists, musicians and writers – including

Royal patronage

In 1897 and 1899, Queen Victoria spent several months at the Hôtel Excelsior Régina in Cimiez, built in her honour, where she occupied the entire west wing. Travelling as Lady Balmoral, the queen socialised with European aristocracy (many of them her relations) and visited the town in a cart drawn by a donkey.

Matisse, Picasso, Stravinsky, Diaghilev, Ernest Hemingway, Henry Miller and Gertrude Stein – also colonised the south, drawn by the southern light and the attractions of the new Mediterranean society.

War and Post-War

During World War II, the Alpes-Maritimes was part of so-called Unoccupied France under the Vichy regime, until occupied by Italian troops in November 1942. They were replaced in September 1943 by German troops after the fall of Mussolini, and liberated in August 1944 by Allied troops from North Africa. The first Cannes Film Festival *(see page 52)* – originally planned for 1939 but postponed due to the war – took place in 1946, heralding a glamorous new image for Cannes – and for Monaco, when film star Grace Kelly married Prince Rainier III in 1956, with Alfred Hitchcock as their witness.

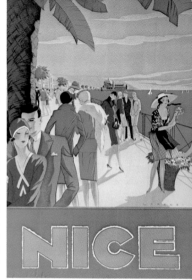

A poster advertising the winter season in 1920s Nice

The post-war period saw all three cities expand enormously, especially Nice, with immigration from North Africa and the return of the *pieds-noirs* (the white colonial population) in the 1960s, following Algerian independence. At the same time there was a change in the type of tourism, already augmented when working people first received paid holidays in 1936, and holidays in the southern sun were no longer the preserve of aristocrats and artists. The birth of mass tourism led to widescale construction all along the coast.

Twentieth-century Nice was also marked by the long reign of mayor Jean Médecin, elected 1928–43 and re-elected from 1947–65, at which point his son, Jacques, succeeded him. Under Jacques Médecin, Nice gained its modern art museum, new theatre, casinos, and the Arenas business district; the town also became the creative centre of a dynamic artistic movement, the Ecole de Nice *(see page 36)*. Adored by many Niçois, Médecin veered close to extreme right politics and was suspected of financial embezzlement, before escaping to Uruguay in 1990 to avoid corruption charges. There (after extradition to France and a brief spell in jail) he died in 1998.

Under Prince Rainier III, Monaco began to take on its present form, with a booming banking sector, skyscrapers replacing 19th-century villas, and an entire district, Fontvieille, constructed on land reclaimed from the sea. Amid suspicions of money laundering, the tax haven's relationship with France and the European Union is not always easy, and Prince Albert II, who succeeded in 2005, has promised greater transparency.

Posing as celebrities at the Palais des Festivals, Cannes

The opening of Nice tramway at the end of 2007 has made the northern outskirts more accessible and spurred the tidying-up of the town centre. The mayor of Nice, Christian Estrosi, elected in 2008, also has ambitious plans for a so-called 'Eco-Vallée' near the airport, with a port, congress centre and football stadium along the River Var.

Historical Landmarks

350BC Phocaeans from Marseille set up trading post of Nikaia.

1st century AD Cemenelum (Cimiez) is capital of the Roman province of Alpes Maritimae.

410 Honorat founds monastery on Lérina island (Ile Saint-Honorat).

972 Guillaume the Liberator expels Saracens from Provence.

1144 Nice becomes a Consulat, ruled by four elected Consuls.

1246 Charles of Anjou marries Béatrice of Provence and becomes Count of Provence.

1297 François Grimaldi takes control of Monaco.

1382 Death of Queen Jeanne. War between supporters of Charles III of Duras and Louis of Anjou.

1388 Nice forms alliance with dukes of Savoy.

1481 Cannes (but not Nice or Monaco) becomes part of France.

1538 Treaty of Nice between François I and Emperor Charles V.

1543 Siege of Nice by French and Turkish armies.

1706 Louis XIV razes Nice's citadel.

1731 English visitors winter at Nice.

1792 French Revolutionary troops take Nice.

1822 Promenade des Anglais constructed.

1834 Lord Henry Brougham discovers Cannes.

1860 Nice joins France after referendum.

1863 Casino opens in Monte Carlo.

1864 The railway reaches Nice from Paris.

1912 Hôtel Carlton opens in Cannes.

1922 First 'Train Bleu' from Calais to the Côte d'Azur.

1931 Hotels in Cannes open in summer for the first time.

1942–3 Nice occupied by Italians.

1944 Liberation of Provence.

1946 First Cannes Film Festival.

1956 Rainier III of Monaco marries Grace Kelly.

2005 Death of Rainier III; Albert II crowned sovereign prince of Monaco.

2007 Nicolas Sarkozy elected president; opening of Nice tramway.

WHERE TO GO

The cities of Nice, Cannes and Monte Carlo dominate one of the most celebrated stretches of coastline in the world, a 50km (30-mile) strip where heavily built-up resorts are interspersed by exclusive peninsulas, home to the happy few, and bordered on the interior by the *arrière-pays* of medieval hill villages and Alpine foothills. If you're not jet-setting by yacht or helicopter between the three, they are well connected by railway, by the A8 *autoroute* and the coastal roads, notably the spectacular trio of corniches between Nice and the Italian frontier, with hairpin bends and stunning sea views.

NICE

With a splendid position curving along the broad sweep of the Baie des Anges, Nice merits its reputation as the Queen of the Riviera or its affectionate Nissart name, Nissa la Bella. Central Nice divides neatly into two parts: Italianate Vieux Nice, beneath the Colline du Château, to the east of the River Paillon; and the elegant New Town, which grew up in the 19th and early 20th centuries behind the Promenade des Anglais to the west. Beyond, Nice extends over a series of hills – Cimiez, Les Baumettes, Piol, Fabron – where urbanisation has largely taken over olive groves and villa gardens.

Vieux Nice

Against a backdrop of colourful houses, Baroque churches and campaniles, the picturesque Old Town mixes Nice at its most traditional, where some elderly residents still speak

Brightly coloured houses line the streets of Vieux Nice

Nissart (an Occitan language related to Provençal) and restaurants serve local specialities that appear not to have changed for generations, alongside bohemian bars, art galleries and clothes shops reflecting the young cosmopolitan set that has rejuvenated the district.

Enter **Vieux Nice** on rue St-François-de-Paule, reached from place Masséna or the Jardin Albert I, passing the town hall, the chic Hôtel Beau Rivage (where Matisse stayed on his first visit in 1917) and the elaborate pink-columned facade of the **Opéra de Nice**, rebuilt in 1884 on the site of the earlier opera house, gutted when the stage curtain caught fire. Across the street, family-run Maison Auer has been producing candied fruits and chocolates since 1820, while Alziari draws connoisseurs for its olive oil, produced at its own mill in the west of the city and sold in decorative tins.

The imposing facade of the Opéra de Nice

Cours Saleya

The street leads into broad **cours Saleya** with brasserie terraces and the colourful flower market (Tue–Sun 6am–5pm) and fruit and vegetable market (Tue–Sun 6am–1pm), held under cheerful striped awnings, where laden stalls reflect the profusion of Riviera produce. Along with the tourists, the market is still frequented by local residents and the town's best chefs.

A cours Saleya flower stall

The market spreads into adjoining place Pierre Gautier, where you'll find many stalls run by local producers, perhaps selling nothing but lemons or delicate orange courgette flowers. On Monday, the fruit and vegetables are replaced by antiques and bric-a-brac stalls. On one side, the **Forum d'Urbanisme et d'Architecture de la Ville de Nice** (Mon–Fri 8.30am–5.30pm, Sat 9am–1pm; free) puts on interesting exhibitions about Nice's architectural heritage and urban projects. At the back of the square, the colonnaded former Palace of the Kings of Sardinia was built by the king of Piedmont when Nice was returned to Sardinia after the Revolution, and now serves as the Préfecture of the Alpes-Maritimes. Next door, the white stone Palais de Justice opens onto place du Palais, facing the russet-coloured **Palazzo Rusca**, a Baroque mansion with impressive triple-storey arcades on one side and an 18th-century clock tower on the other. There is a second-hand book market on the square on the first and third Saturday of each month.

Cours Saleya is bordered on the sea side by **Les Ponchettes**, a double alley of low fishermen's cottages, with archways

Vieux Nice architecture

leading through to quai des Etats-Unis. Amid restaurants and a couple of exclusive shops, two vaulted halls play host to municipal exhibitions of contemporary art: **Galerie des Ponchettes** and **Galerie de la Marine** (both Tue–Sun 10am–6pm; free).

About halfway along cours Saleya, the **Chapelle de la Miséricorde** (Tue 2.30–6pm) is generally considered the finest of all Nice's Baroque interiors. It belongs to the *pénitents noirs*, one of the religious lay fraternities that still thrives in the town, but is only open for extremely limited hours. Further along, on the corner with rue de la Poissonnerie, is the **Adam and Eve house**, one of the oldest buildings in the city, decorated with a Naïve 16th-century relief of Adam and Eve in the Garden of Eden.

Heart of the Old Town

However, it is in the grid of narrow, shady streets behind cours Saleya where you get a real feel for the atmosphere of Vieux Nice. Although the population started moving down from Castle Hill in the 13th century, the town was almost entirely reconstructed in the 17th and 18th centuries, giving it much the appearance it has today: for the most part tall simple facades in tones of yellow and orange, punctuated by Baroque churches and the occasional fine carved doorway.

In the heart of Vieux Nice, lively **place Rossetti** has a dual appeal: the ice creams and sorbets of Fenocchio, where more than 90 flavours range from classic coffee and pistachio to rose, pina colada and beer; and the sculpted facade of **Sainte-Réparate cathedral** (daily 9am–noon, 2–6pm), built on a cruciform plan in the 1650s. It is dedicated to early Christian martyr Saint Reparata, the city's patron saint, whose body, accompanied by two angels (hence the name Baie des Anges) is said to have arrived here by boat after drifting across the Mediterranean from Palestine, where she had been decapitated at the age of 15. Despite its impressive painted dome over the transept and numerous Baroque side chapels, the Niçois prefer the cheerful little **Eglise Sainte-Rita** (daily 7am–noon, 2.30–6.30pm) on rue de la Poissonnerie, an intimate gem, with a skylit half-dome and profusion of sculpted saints, barley-sugar columns and sunbursts. Take a look also at the arcaded Loggia Communale, dating from 1574, around the corner on rue de la Préfecture.

Inside Sainte-Réparate

From here, rue Droite, once the main thoroughfare, leads to the Eglise Saint-Jacques or **Eglise du Gésu** (daily 3–6pm), built by the Jesuit order in 1607. It set the model for Nice's Baroque churches, with its single-naved interior full of stucco cherubs and stripy painted marble, although the blue-and-white classical facade is a later reworking. Further up the street at No. 15 is the **Palais Lascaris** (Wed–Mon

10am–noon, 2–6pm; free), the 17th-century Genoese-style mansion of the Lascaris-Ventimille family and Nice's grandest secular Baroque building. The sober street facade does not prepare you for the splendour of the interior, with its magnificent vaulted stairway, decorated with sculptures and frescoed grotesques. On the second floor, staterooms, furnished with Baroque furniture and tapestries, have spectacular painted ceilings with mythological scenes: *Venus and Adonis*, the *Abduction of Psyche* and the *Fall of Phaethon*, where youth and horses tumble from the sky amid a mass of swirling clouds. The first floor has been renovated to house the town's extensive collection of 18th- and 19th-century musical instruments. Don't miss the period pharmacy on the right of the entrance, with wooden shelves and majolica jars.

Higher up, rue Droite runs into rue St-François and the place St-François, home to a small fish market every morning except Monday. The 17th-century former Palais Communal is now a trades union building. Further along, rue Parolière is busy with food shops and typical Niçois bistros, while on the corner of rue Miralheti, customers queue up for plastic plates of *socca (see page 98)* and other Niçois snacks at ever-popular Chez René Socca.

On the northern edge of Vieux Nice, the handsome **place Garibaldi**, with arcaded facades and the neoclassical Chapelle du Saint-Sépulcre, was laid out in the 1780s by the king of Sardinia, Victor-Amédée, to create a monumental entry to the town on the completion

Independence hero

Giuseppe Garibaldi, hero of Italian independence, was actually born in Nice in 1807. Although as a convinced republican he helped the French in the Franco-Prussian war of 1870, he had earlier opposed the attachment of Nice to France, which is said to be why his statue in place Garibaldi faces towards Italy.

Musicians charm the crowds in Vieux Nice

of the royal carriageway from Turin. Originally called Piazza Vittoria, it was renamed in honour of the Nice-born hero of Italian reunification whose statue stands in the middle. Note that Garibaldi is facing Italy, while beneath him two bronze women carry a baby, presumably the infant nation. On one side of the square, the Café de Turin is an institution for shellfish-lovers. Excavations during the construction of the tramway revealed part of the antique port under the square, long considered a frontier between aristocratic Nice to the west and poorer working-class Nice to the east.

The Colline du Château

Reached by assorted steep stairways from Vieux Nice, by tourist train from the quay in front of Jardin Albert I, by lift (daily summer 9.30am–7pm, winter 10am–5.30pm; charge) or by stairs at the end of quai des Etats-Unis, the **Colline du Château** was for centuries the heart of the medieval city that

Midday cannon shot

Every day at noon, a resounding boom announces the midday cannon shot fired from the Colline du Château. The tradition was inaugurated by Sir Thomas Coventry-More in the 1860s to ensure that his forgetful wife returned home in time to prepare lunch, and was perpetuated by the municipality in 1871.

grew up around the castle, before the population moved down to the plain. Today nothing remains of the citadel, razed in 1706 on orders of Louis XIV, but the remaining mound provides a shady interlude on hot summer days, and plenty of gorgeous views over the bay and the Old Town's pantiled roofs and campaniles. Follow the sound of water up to the cascade that tumbles dramatically over a man-made lump of rock. Below lie an amphitheatre, a café, children's playgrounds and the poorly indicated ruins of the medieval cathedral and the residential district destroyed in the siege of 1691. Slightly down the hill to the north are two graveyards: the **Jewish cemetery** with its funerary stelae, and the **Catholic cemetery** (which also includes Orthodox and Protestant tombs of some of the town's noble émigrés), which resembles a miniature city with gravel paths and a forest of elaborate 19th-century monuments to Niçois notables. Overlooking the sea, at the top of the lift is the solid round **Tour Bellanda** (Tue–Sun 10am–6pm), a mock fortification reconstructed in the 19th century, where Hector Berlioz lived while composing his *King Lear Overture*. It is currently being converted to hold a display about the history of Castle Hill.

The Vieux Port

Back at sea level, quai Rauba Capéu (Nissart for 'flying hat', because of the breeze) curves around the castle mound past a striking World War I war memorial set into its cliff face, to the picturesque **Vieux Port.** The port can also be reached from place Garibaldi along rue Ségurane, known for its cluster of antiques dealers and bric-a-brac shops. Framed by the castle hill on one side and Mont Boron on the other, the Bassin Lympia was dug out in the late 18th century (before that fishing boats were simply pulled up on the shore and Nice's main port was at nearby Villefranche-sur-Mer). At the same time, beautiful arcaded **place Ile de Beauté** was built along the north side in Genoese fashion, with deep-red facades and ornate *trompe l'œil* window frames, on either side of the neoclassical sailors' church **Eglise Notre-Dame du Port**. More tranquil than Vieux Nice, the restaurants along the eastern quay, mostly specialising in fish, are popular. Departure point for ferries to Corsica, the port has recently been the subject of debate over controversial plans to expand it for giant cruise ships, but it has now been decided to leave

The view over the Vieux Port from the Colline du Château

it as a yachting marina and construct a new commercial port on the western side of town.

Just east of the port on boulevard Carnot at the start of the Basse Corniche is a curious but fascinating museum, at the bottom of an apartment block on the very spot at the foot of Mont Boron where a tribe of elephant-hunters briefly camped on the beach 400,000 years ago in the Middle Pleistocene period, when the sea level was 26 metres (84ft) higher than today. This is the **Musée de Paléontologie Humaine de Terra Amata** (Tue–Sun 10am–6pm; free; www.musee-terra-amata.org). When the site was discovered in 1966, archaeologists worked day and night for five weeks before it was built on. The centrepiece is a large cast made of the ground, showing traces of tools, debris, animal bones and even a footprint left behind, while other exhibits include axeheads, flint tools and a reconstructed twig hut.

Beyond here wooded Mont Boron conceals luxurious residences and 11km (7 miles) of public footpaths. At the top of the hill, the 19th-century military fort is set to be transformed into an architecture centre by architect Jean Nouvel.

Figures atop metal poles preside over place Masséna

Promenade du Paillon

Created when the River Paillon was covered over as a hygiene measure in the 19th century, the **promenade du Paillon** marks the divide between Vieux Nice on one side and the New Town on the other. At its centre, **place Masséna** forms the symbolic heart of Nice, with elegant arcaded facades in Pompeian red, laid out in the 1840s as

Elegant place Masséna

part of the urbanisation plan of the Consiglio d'Ornato, the council designated by King Charles-Albert in Turin to mastermind the expansion of the city. Long a traffic-clogged junction, the square was beautifully repaved and pedestrianised for the opening of the tramway in 2007, with the installation of an artwork by Spanish artist Jaume Plensa, with seven resin figures atop tall metal poles, which symbolise the different continents and are illuminated in a colourful glow at night.

Towards the sea, the pleasant shady **Jardin Albert I** contains the Théâtre de Verdure, an outdoor amphitheatre used for summer concerts, and a massive bronze arc sculpture by Bernar Venet that seems to float over the lawn.

Promenades des Arts

On the other side of place Masséna, the promenade du Paillon leads to the **promenades des Arts**, created in the 1980s by mayor Jacques Médecin as part of his ambitious cultural programme. Designed by architects Yves Bayard and Henri Vidal, the Carrara marble complex comprises the Théâtre National de Nice, a terrace with sculptures by Calder, Borovsky and Niki de Saint Phalle's mosaic Loch Ness Monster fountain, and the **Musée d'Art Moderne et Contemporain** (MAMAC; Tue–Sun 10am–6pm; free; www.mamac-nice.org). The building looks rather harsh from outside but the galleries inside, where four wings are connected by glass bridges, provide a luminous setting for works from the 1960s to the present. The museum's strength lies in its collection of the Ecole de Nice, including an entire room of

The Ecole de Nice

In the late 1950s and 1960s, Nice shot to the forefront of artistic creation in France, around the trio Yves Klein, Arman and Martial Raysse, championed by critic Pierre Restany, and later joined by César, Sosno, Ben, Niki de Saint Phalle and Robert Malaval. Although associated with Nouveau Réalisme (the French equivalent of Pop Art), Fluxus and Supports-Surfaces, the Ecole de Nice was more about a sense of energy and sometimes anarchist attitudes than a stylistic school. The pivotal figure was Yves Klein (1928–62), who combined painting and art actions in his famous monochromes in trademark IKB (International Klein Blue), and *anthropométries*, where female models covered in paint were rolled like a living paintbrush over the canvas. Unlike most earlier modern artists who found inspiration in the south, this was a home-grown movement: Klein, Arman and Malaval were born in Nice, César and Sosno in Marseille, Raysse at Golfe Juan. As Klein remarked in 1947: 'Even if we, the artists of Nice, are always on holiday, we are not tourists. That is the essential point. Tourists come here for the holidays; as for us, we live in this holiday land, which is what gives us our touch of madness. We amuse ourselves without thinking about religion or art or science.'

Yves Klein's monochromes, blue sponges and fire paintings, works by Ben, Raysse, Malaval and Christo, Arman's accumulations and cut-up musical instruments and an exceptional donation by Niki de Saint Phalle, which is complemented by parallel movements in American Pop Art, including works by Warhol, Lichtenstein and Rauschenberg.

Ringing the changes at the MAMAC

Across the street on boulevard Risso, the **Muséum d'Histoire Naturelle** (Tue–Sun 10am–6pm; free; www.mhnnice.org) harks back to a decidedly different era, with stuffed birds, botanical specimens and minerals illustrating the Mediterranean habitat and a display of Australasian and Polynesian shells and coral.

To the north, the promenade des Arts' latest addition is heralded by the bizarre vision of the *Tête Carrée*, a massive 30-metre (96ft) high head by sculptor Sacha Sosno, described by the artist as 'an inhabited sculpture', which morphs into a cube containing the offices of the **Bibliothèque Louis Nucéra** (public library), opened in 2002 – the books and public entrance are actually underground. Beyond, before the river finally resurfaces, are the **Acropolis** congress and exhibition centres, opened in the 1980s, making Nice a major venue for international trade fairs and conferences.

The New Town

West of the Paillon, the New Town grew up in the 19th and early 20th centuries behind the promenade des Anglais, laid out in a grid of broad avenues and garden squares roughly following the plan conceived by the Consiglio d'Ornato *(see page 35)*, planted with the exotic palms, citrus trees and bougainvillaea that have acclimatised in the south of France. After the narrow streets and deep shadows of Vieux Nice, the atmosphere here is airy and bright. Although the street plan is regular, the architecture is anything but, making this area a delight for walkers.

Promenade des Anglais

With blue chairs, white pergolas, palm trees and Belle Epoque architecture, the **promenade des Anglais** has come to symbolise the elegance of Nice – not bad for

Sunbathers on a stretch of public beach

what began in 1822 as an employment exercise, when the Reverend Lewis Way opened a public subscription to construct a new footpath along the shore, linking the Old Town to the British colony that had settled on the hills further west. The promenade took on its present appearance in the 1930s when the thoroughfare was widened. Despite busy traffic, it remains a favourite place to walk, not just for the sea views but for the diversity of those who use it, from roller bladers to elderly ladies, and for the splendour of its grand hotels, although few restaurants or boutiques line the promenade.

Running westwards from Jardin Albert I, where the Méridien Nice and neighbouring Casino Ruhl controversially replaced the old Hôtel Ruhl in the 1970s, admire the Art Deco facade of the **Palais de la Méditerranée** at No. 15. Built in 1929 for American millionaire Frank Jay Gould, it epitomised 1930s glamour with a casino, theatre, restaurant and cocktail bar. The Palais closed in 1978 and was gutted before reopening with a modern hotel, apartments and casino behind the listed facade. At No. 27, the pink stucco Westminster still has its grandiose reception rooms, while Hôtel West End (No. 31) was the first of the promenade's grand hotels, opened in 1855.

Next door, set back from the promenade at the rear of a luscious garden laid out by Edouard André, the **Musée d'Art et d'Histoire Palais Masséna** (Wed–Mon 10am–6pm; free), built in 1898 for Prince Victor Masséna, grandson of one of

Beaches for All

With 15 beach concessions running along the Baie des Anges, Nice's private beaches are about much more than just swimming and sun-bathing, although the sun loungers (matelas) can be a boon on the uncomfortable pebbles. **Castel Plage** on quai des Etats-Unis at the eastern end of the Baie des Anges calls itself 'the beautiful beach for beautiful people' and likes to promote its arty image with chess matches and art exhibitions; **Beau Rivage**, belonging to the elegant Vieux Nice hotel, has a vast restaurant serving a modern Med-Asian fusion cuisine, with a DJ in the afternoons and jazz on Sundays; **Blue Beach** near the Hôtel West End is a chic place to dine by night and a child-friendly beach by day, with table tennis, a popular seawater pool for kids and water sports next door; while trendy new **Hi Beach**, designed by Matali Crasset, is split into lifestyle zones – Play for families, with sandpit and anti-UV cabins for babies; Relax, with plants and hammocks; Energy around the bar – plus computers, books and magazines, yoga and massages, solar-powered showers and a restaurant and sushi bar overseen by acclaimed chef Keisuke Matsushima.

Napoleon's generals, has been renovated as a museum devoted to the Belle Epoque past. On the ground floor are grandiose reception rooms, with Empire furniture, sumptuous inlaid panelling and a full-length portrait of Napoleon. Upstairs, the aristocrats, artists and intellectuals who shaped 19th-century Nice are portrayed in an eclectic array of portraits, paintings, documents and memorabilia, including the cloak worn by Josephine when Napoleon was crowned king of Naples, and paintings of Old Nice. Among curiosities are a poster, in French and Italian, calling citizens to vote in the referendum for Nice to rejoin France in April 1860.

The opulent Hôtel Negresco is a Nice institution

On the other side, Nice's grandest hotel, the **Hôtel Negresco**, is an institution with its pink-and-green cupola and uniformed doormen. Designed by Edouard Niermans, with a glazed *verrière* by Gustave Eiffel over the salon, it was one of the most modern hotels in the world when it opened in 1913, with lavish bathrooms and telephones in the rooms; but with the outbreak of war in 1914 it was transformed into a hospital and Romanian owner Henri Negresco was ruined. Still a favourite with politicians and film stars, the hotel is endearingly idiosyncratic, with antique furniture, carousel horses and a kitsch souvenir shop.

Across the New Town

Parallel to the promenade des Anglais, broad **avenue Victor Hugo** is a panorama of New Town architecture, from classical villas with wrought-iron balconies and a neo-Gothic church to carved friezes, ornate Belle Epoque rotundas, Art Deco mansion blocks and stream-lined 1950s zigzags. Between here and the station is the quieter **Musicians' Quarter**, with streets named after composers and the circular Escu-rial Art Deco apartment block. On the eastward continuation of avenue Victor Hugo, the **Théâtre de la Photographie et de l'Image** (27 boulevard Debouchage; Tue–Sun 10am–6pm; free; www.tpi-nice.org) stages excellent photographic exhibitions. The building itself is worth a look, with a decorative theatre and neo-Renaissance ceilings.

> ### Bank heist
>
> France's biggest ever bank heist took place at the Société Générale on avenue Jean Médecin in 1976, when Albert Spaggiari climbed through the sewers and tunnelled into the vault, coolly leaving with 50 million francs (c.24 million euros). Arrested months later, he escaped from police custody to South America, publishing his autobiography and frater-nising with Ronnie Biggs.

Just off place Masséna, the **'Carré d'Or'**, formed by avenues de Suède and Verdun, rue Masséna and rue Paradis (and its extension, rue Alphonse Karr), is home to Nice's smartest clothes shops. Pedestrianised rue Masséna and adjoining rue de France form an animated hub with chain stores and pizzerias. **Avenue Jean Médecin**, the busy tree-lined shopping street that runs north from Masséna towards the station, has slid downmarket since it was laid out on the Haussmannian model with grand department stores, banks and opulent cafés. However, with the reduction of traffic since the opening of the tramway and the probability that the street will soon be pedestrianised, it may rediscover its aura of old.

Western Nice

On the Beaumettes hill, the **Musée des Beaux-Arts de Nice** (33 avenue des Baumettes; Tue–Sun 10am–6pm; free; www.musee-beaux-arts-nice.org) occupies an extravagant mansion built in 1878 for the Ukrainian Princess Elisabeth Kotschoubey, which gives some idea of the grandeur in which the foreign aristocracy lived. Downstairs, the Old Masters section ranges from medieval religious panel paintings to 18th-century canvases by Natoire and Van Loo. Look out for two highly detailed allegorical landscapes of Water and Earth by 'Velvet' Brueghel, swarming with fantastical animals and birds, and a bravura fantasy portrait by Fragonard. At the top of the stairs, past plaster studies by Carpeaux, the 19th- and 20th-century collections include romantic pastels by Jules Cheret, best-known as a decorator and poster artist, Symbolist paintings by Gustave-Adolphe Mossa, the museum's first curator, Impressionist works by Monet and Sisley, striking portraits by Kees van Dongen, a room of cheerful seaside scenes by Raoul Dufy, and numerous paintings by Russian artist and diarist Marie Bashkirtseff. The Baumettes hill itself is worth a wander for the villas erected by British and Russian aristocrats, including the pink mock-medieval **Château des Ollières** and the **Château de la Tour**.

A take on the Three Graces at the Musée des Beaux-Arts

Further west, in a villa owned by perfumier François Coty in the 1920s, is the **Musée International d'Art Naïf Anatole Jakovsky** (avenue Val-Marie; Wed–Mon 10am–6pm; free), centred around a vast collection of Naïve art donated by the

The Musée des Beaux-Arts' grandiose exterior

Romanian art critic Anatole Jakovsky, one of the first, along with artist Jean Dubuffet, to admire the colourful meticulous works by these self-taught artists. The collection includes a portrait by Le Douanier Rousseau, obsessively detailed paintings of Paris monuments by Louis Vivin, and other major Naïve artists including Jules Lefranc, Séraphine, Rimbert, Bombois, as well as the American Grandma Moses.

Parc Floral Phoenix

At the very westernmost end of the promenade des Anglais, just before the airport and the modern Arenas business district, **Parc Floral Phoenix** (daily Apr–Sept 9.30am–7.30pm, Oct–Mar 9.30am–6pm; charge) is an imaginative modern botanical garden that is enjoyable for families and plant-lovers. Around the garden you'll find streams with stepping stones, aviaries with cranes, parrots and birds of prey, prairie dogs, an otter pool and crested porcupines. The vast polygonal, 25-metre (82ft) high glasshouse – one of the largest in Europe – is a hothouse wonderland, where different zones recreate different tropical and desert climates, with magnificent palms, tree ferns and orchids, and habitats populated by giant iguanas, carp and flamingos, as well as an aquarium and tanks of tarantulas. Sitting in the lake by the entrance to the park is the **Musée des Arts Asiatiques** (Wed–Mon May–mid-Oct 10am–6pm, mid-Oct–May 10am–5pm; free; www.arts-asiatiques.com), a striking geometrical building symbolising Earth and Sky, designed by Japanese architect Kenzo Tange. The small but high-quality collection of art from China, Japan, India and Cambodia includes ornate samurai swords and ancient Chinese bronzes and terracottas. There is an adjoining teahouse, where the Japanese tea ceremony is performed on certain weekends.

North of the Station

The arrival of the railway from Paris in 1864 hastened Nice's rise as a destination for *le tout Europe*, with a station in Louis XIII-style brick and stone facings in a new district north of the centre – what is now a typical station hinterland of cheap hotels and ethnic eateries. To the west across boulevard Gambetta, in what was once the heart of the Russian district, the **Cathédrale Orthodoxe Russe Saint-Nicolas** (boulevard Tzarewitch; Mon–Sat 9am–noon, 2.30–6pm, Sun 2.30–6pm, Oct–May until 5pm; charge), with five onion domes and glazed tiles, is a surreal apparition amid the modern apartment blocks. Inspired by St Basil's in Moscow and inaugurated in 1912, the largest Russian Orthodox church outside Russia – and single most visited sight in Nice – was commissioned by the Tsarina Maria Feodorovna, mother of Tsar Nicolas II, when an earlier church on rue Longchamp became too small for the growing Russian community. The atmospheric interior, laden with icons, carvings and frescoes, contains a magnificent gilded repoussé copper iconostasis (the screen that separates the congregation from the sanctuary reserved for the clergy). In the grounds is a small chapel built on the spot where Grand Duke Nicolas Alexandrovich, son of Alexander II, died in 1865 aged 21. Nearby on avenue Paul Arène, you can also spot the 1902 Hôtel du Parc Impérial, which was originally destined for Russian families wintering in the town but became a lycée after World War I.

On avenue Bourriglione, the extraordinary **Eglise Jeanne d'Arc** is exotic in a different way. An architectural one-off, the avant-garde white concrete church designed in the 1930s by Jacques Droz resembles a box of eggs with its cluster of ovoid domes. The parabolic interior is decorated with murals by Eugène Klementieff and stylised concrete sculptures of Joan of Arc and the Crucifixion by Carlo Sarrabezolles, a pioneer in sculpting directly into wet concrete. Further north, in a 17th-century Italianate villa, largely disguised by a radical raw concrete and pebble extension, the **Villa Arson, Centre National d'Art Contemporain** (20 avenue Stéphen Liégeard; Wed–Mon 2–6pm; free; www.villa-arson.org) is home to one of France's most adventurous art schools and exhibition centres.

The onion-domed Russian Orthodox Cathedral

Enjoying a leisurely game of *pétanque* in Cimiez

Cimiez

Smart residential Cimiez is where Nice feels closest to its Belle Epoque spirit. Northeast of the centre by boulevard Carabacel and boulevard de Cimiez, this is a district of winding streets that meander uphill, lined with stucco villas amid lush gardens and palm trees. On avenue Docteur Menard is the **Musée National Marc Chagall** (Wed–Mon 10am–6pm; charge; www.musee-chagall.fr), where paintings by Chagall are set off by the beautifully designed low modern building and surrounding Mediterranean garden. Inaugurated in 1973, it was the first time a national museum in France had been devoted to a living artist. It was created for his series of 17 scenes from the Old Testament, which reveal Chagall's unique ability to combine colour and narrative with a personal iconography. In another room are five rose-tinted paintings of the canticles dedicated to 'Vava', his wife Valentina Brodsky, and in the auditorium are three intense stained-glass windows and related studies depicting *The Creation of the World*.

Almost across the street, on boulevard de Cimiez , the fine Belle Epoque **Villa Paradiso** now belongs to the town's education service, but is surrounded by pretty public gardens. Further up the boulevard you can spot the White Palace and the Alhambra (distinguished by its two mosque-like minarets), grand former hotels built in the days before sea bathing became popular, when this was the most fashionable part of town to stay.

At the top of the boulevard de Cimiez, the ornate **Hôtel Excelsior Régina**, by architect Biasini, was built in 1896 in anticipation of a visit by Queen Victoria. The queen in fact stayed here twice, occupying the entire west wing with a suite of more than 70 rooms, an event commemorated in the crown over the entrance and a marble statue outside. Converted into apartments in the 1930s, this is where Matisse lived at the end of his life, sketching on the ceiling from his bed with a brush attached to a long pole.

Roman Remains

Across the street are the scant remains (entrance tunnels, a few tiers of seats) of the **Roman amphitheatre**, which once seated 5,000 people and is now used for the Nice Jazz Festival each summer *(see page 86)*. To get a clearer idea of Nice's Roman incarnation as the city of Cemenelum, visit the adjacent **Musée Archéologique** (Wed–Mon 10am–

Nice Observatory

Charles Garnier and Gustave Eiffel, two of the 19th century's greatest architects and engineers, collaborated in the construction of Nice Observatory on Mont Gros, east of the city above the Saint-Roch district. Still at the cutting edge of research, it is open for guided visits (Wed, Sat 2.45pm; charge; www.obs-nice.fr).

6pm; free), which has displays of statues, glassware and jewellery excavated in the area and, in the basement, sarcophagi and inscribed stelae from a nearby necropolis, as well as the chance to try out some Roman board games.

The most interesting part of the museum is the archaeological site outside, where extensive remains include some imposing walls and canals and pieces of hypocaust (the underfloor heating system) from three bathing complexes dating from Cemenelum's 3rd-century heyday, as well as a 5th-century palaeo-Christian baptistery.

Homage to Matisse

Behind the ruins, you can spot the rust-coloured Genoese villa that houses the **Musée Matisse** (164 avenue des Arènes; Wed–Mon 10am–6pm; free; www.musee-matisse-nice.org), though the entrance is around the corner, reached through a grove of ancient olive trees. The extensive collection hung around the house and in the discreet underground modern extension spans the artist's entire career from early paintings of the 1890s to his late paper cut-outs, allowing one to see how he assimilated such inspirations as Riviera sunlight, patterned textiles, classical sculpture and voyages to North Africa and Tahiti.

Highlights include Fauve portraits, the vibrant *Still Life with Grenadines*, small oil studies for different versions of *La Danse*, *Odalesque au Coffret Rouge*, a series of small bronze heads of *Jeannette*, and the colourful late cut-out *Flowers and Fruit*, made in 1953.

Pay further homage to Matisse in the simple slab-like tomb that sits on its own terrace in the gardens of the **Cimiez Cemetery** just up the road, the burial place for many British and Russian aristocrats. Painter Raoul Dufy is also buried here, although on the other side of the cemetery. You can admire fine views of the hills of Nice and down to the coast

The rust-coloured facade of the Musée Matisse

from the adjoining rose garden before visiting the **Eglise Franciscain** (Mon–Sat 10am–noon, 3–6pm; free). Although the church facade has been rebuilt in a rather garish style, the interior is a simple Gothic structure with walls and vault entirely covered in murals, and a Baroque retable. The church contains three paintings by local master Ludovico Bréa *(see page 16)*: a *Pièta* triptych from around 1475, a *Crucifixion* of 1512 and a late *Deposition* attributed to Bréa, dating from around 1520. It is interesting to contrast the Gothic emotion depicted in the early angular *Pièta* with the luminosity and symmetrical layout of the later *Crucifixion*, with its solidly posed figures and perspective that carries to a far-off landscape.

Upstairs, the monastic buildings contain a small museum presenting the history of the Franciscan order in Nice, through paintings, manuscripts, a reconstituted monk's cell and a small, simple chapel.

Taking it easy on La Croisette

CANNES

Cannes is the glamour capital of the Alpes-Maritimes, a place for hedonists to succumb to the indulgence of sun, sand, shopping and more shopping. Yet unlike many Riviera resorts, it does qualify as a real town with an all-year population where, alongside some of the glitziest shops in the world, the Old Town still has the allure of a Provençal village, and men play *boules* under the trees in front of the town hall.

By far the most scenic way to arrive in Cannes is from the west along the Corniche de l'Estérel, although traffic is often nose to tail during the holiday season. If you are approaching from the *autoroute*, the road descends to the coast from Le Cannet by boulevard Carnot, past modern apartment blocks and some fine Belle Epoque buildings, including the Palais de Justice and the Hôtel Cavendish, to arrive at the Palais des Festivals.

Sitting on the seafront between the Old Port and La Croisette, the **Palais des Festivals** (www.palaisdesfestivals. com) is the symbol of film festival glamour. Although the building itself is an entirely uninspiring piece of 1980s architecture, nicknamed 'the bunker', it is part of the Cannes Festival myth, as epitomised by the famous walk up *les marches* – the steps leading to the grand auditorium – and the trail of handprints made by film stars and directors in the terracotta pavement outside. With its 18 auditoria, however, the Palais is used for numerous events – music industry awards, advertising and property development fairs, luxury shopping and tourism conventions, rock concerts and chess tournaments. The building also contains the Casino Croisette, the tourist office and the Rotonde de Lérins extension overlooking the sea.

La Croisette

Running east along the bay from the Palais, **La Croisette**, Cannes's palm tree-lined seafront promenade, marked the resort's social ascension in the early 20th century with a trio of legendary palace hotels: the **Majestic**, opened in 1926, the ornate **Carlton**, opened in 1912, with two cupolas, supposedly modelled on the breasts of celebrated courtesan La Belle Otero, and the Art Deco **Martinez**, built by Emmanuel Martinez, who modestly named it after himself. When it opened in 1929, just in time for the transition to the summer season, it was France's largest hotel, with 476 spacious master bedrooms and 56 for clients' personal staff.

La Croisette is still a hub of activity, animated by the parade of open-top cars and illuminated at night for an evening promenade. In summer, the long sandy beach is almost entirely taken up by private beach concessions, with restaurants, deckchairs and jetties for parascending and water-skiing, although there is a small, crowded and fuel-fume-polluted public section between the Majestic jetty and the Palais des Festivals. And where else could you walk along the seafront on New Year's Eve and see, on one side, women promenading in their fur coats and, on the other, leathery-skinned elderly ladies bronzing in bikinis?

The first section of La Croisette is home to the smartest designer labels and jewellers, fun for window-shopping even if you're not in the market for evening gowns and diamond tiaras. Set amid lawns halfway along at No. 47, dwarfed by many of its neighbours, **La Malmaison** (10am–1pm, 2.30–6.30pm; charge) is the last Belle Epoque remnant of the Grand Hôtel, staging a mixed bag of art exhibitions.

Cannes Film Festival

For 10 days in May, Cannes becomes capital of world cinema. Couturiers lend actresses their most extravagant creations, paparazzi snap cast and directors climbing *les marches* of the Palais des Festivals, fans press behind the barriers in hope of a signature, 4,000 journalists try to get slots in the interview room and Paris's trendiest nightclubs decamp south. Launched in the 1930s, when the Venice Film Festival was tainted by Fascism, Cannes was chosen for its sunny location and its promise to build a special auditorium. In the event, war broke out and the first festival was held in 1946 in the municipal casino. Over the years, the festival has spawned the International Critics' Week and Directors' Fortnight, as well as the vast film market dealings that go on around the port. Although a strictly professional event, the organisers have made some concessions to the public with the Cinéma de la Plage open-air screenings.

The festival sticks determinedly to its art-movie reputation. Directors like Ken Loach and the Belgian Dardenne brothers are regulars; big-budget Hollywood blockbusters tend to be screened out of competition, and the selection remains wildly international – films from Mexico, Iran and Romania all get a look in. There are occasionally some heart-warming surprises – in 2008 the Palme d'Or went to Laurent Cantet's *The Class*, acted by a cast of Paris schoolkids (www.festival-cannes.fr).

Further along, the villas have largely been replaced by apartment buildings, with sun-catching balconies. At the east end, beyond pine-shaded gardens and the Port Canto yachting marina, La Croisette terminates at the Pointe de la Croisette promontory, where the **Palm Beach Casino**, built in 1929 and reopened in 2002 after several years' closure, contains a restaurant, gaming rooms, nightclub and an outdoor casino in summer.

The festival action unfolds at the Palais des Festivals

Running parallel to La Croisette, **rue d'Antibes**, which follows the trace of the old royal road between Toulon and Antibes, is almost entirely devoted to the art of shopping, where mainstream fashion chains mix with more cutting-edge stores. Amid the storefronts, if you look up, is some fine late 19th-century architecture, with sculptures and wrought-iron decoration. At night, the block formed by rue des Frères Pradignac, rue du Commandant André and rue Dr Monod is a focus for nightlife, with its restaurants and lounge bars.

The Port Vieux and Marché Forville

West of the Palais des Festivals is the **Port Vieux**, reconstructed in the 19th century to meet the demands of its new British visitors. Today, a few surviving fishing boats sit somewhat incongruously among the luxury yachts, surrounded by the colour-washed facades of the quai St-Pierre and brasseries, bars and shellfish restaurants of avenue Félix Faure. Next to the pompous 19th-century town hall, the plane tree-lined **Allées de la Liberté** contain a vintage bandstand, *pétanque* pitches and a flower market. In the adjoining square, on a plinth above a very British-looking lion is a statue of Lord Henry Brougham, credited with discovering Cannes for the British after spending a night here in 1834 *(see page 18)*. Nearby, rue du Bivouac Napoléon recalls another visitor, who camped here after landing at Golfe-Juan on 1 March 1815, when he escaped from exile on Elba.

Behind the port, pedestrianised rue Meynadier is lined with inexpensive clothes and shoe stores at one end, simple restaurants, bars and food shops at the other, while a street back, **Marché Forville** (summer daily 7am–1pm, winter Tue–Sun) covered market provides a taste of the 'real Cannes' – though you have to arrive early to find what's left of the local catch: sardines, tiny sea bream and little rockfish. In summer, stalls are a tempting feast of tomatoes, courgettes, small aubergines, hot little red peppers, melons, peaches and green figs.

Restaurants in Le Suquet

Le Suquet

Before the arrival of the British in the 19th century, Le Suquet was pretty much all there was of Cannes: a few picturesque streets and stepped alleyways of tall yellow-and-pink houses winding up the hill around the fortress constructed by the monks of Lérins. Quiet and villagey by day, Le Suquet is particularly lively at night, when visitors flock to the bars and restaurants on rue St-Antoine and its con-

A charming side street

tinuation, rue du Suquet. At the very top, beyond the 16th-century church of **Notre-Dame d'Espérance**, whose parvis is used for open-air concerts in summer, shady place de la Castre offers a fine view from the ramparts. Entered through a pretty garden, the cool, whitewashed rooms of the former castle now contain the **Musée de la Castre** (July–Aug daily 10am–7pm, Apr–June, Sept Tue–Sun 10am–1pm, 2–6pm, Oct–Mar Tue–Sun 10am–1pm, 2–5pm; charge), a surprising ethnographic collection donated by the Dutch Baron Lycklama in 1877. An eclectic array of masks, headdresses, statues and ceremonial daggers from Tibet, Nepal and Ladakh, bone carvings from Alaska, animal-shaped jugs from Latin America and archaeological finds from ancient Egypt, Cyprus and Mesopotamia are complemented by a couple of rooms of paintings by Orientalist and Provençal painters. From the courtyard you can climb 109 narrow steps up the 11th-century **Tour du Suquet** for panoramic views over the town, port and bay.

Mérimée's verdict

'The English who have built here deserve to be impaled for the architecture they have brought into this beautiful country. You cannot imagine how distressed I am to see these stage-set castles posed on these lovely hills.'

La Croix des Gardes

West of the port, the **Plage du Midi**, with the railway running along the side, is less chic than La Croisette, but its largely public beach makes it a better bet if you're not going to one of the private establishments. Back on the other side of the railway, **La Croix des Gardes** district is where many British settlers built their residences in a variety of styles ranging from Palladian villas to rustic cottages and crenellated castles, following on from Lord Brougham, whose neoclassical Villa Eléonore stands on avenue Docteur Picaud. Most are now private apartments only glimpsed from the road amid luxuriant gardens, but you can see the **Château de la Tour** on avenue Font de Veyre (now a hotel) and the **Villa Rothschild** (1 avenue Jean de Noailles), built in 1881 for the Baronne de Rothschild, and now the municipal library, whose gardens planted with palms, catalpas and other exotic species have become a pleasant public park. At the top of the hill, boulevard Leader and avenue de Noailles emerge in a surprisingly wild protected nature area, crossed by several footpaths, and marked at the top by a glistening steel cross.

Prosper Mérimée (1803–70), novelist and inspector of historic monuments, was another winter visitor, staying with English sisters Emma and Fanny Lagdon. He preferred Cannes to Nice, which he thought as crowded as Paris, but detested many of the new buildings *(see panel)*. He is buried alongside many British settlers, including Lord Brougham, and numerous Russian aristocrats and artists, in the **Cimetière du Grand Jas**, which descends in scenic terraces down the eastern flank of the hill.

Le Cannet

Reached up boulevard Carnot, on the hill above Cannes, the suburb of Le Cannet was originally settled by Italian immigrants brought here by the monks of Lérins in the 16th century to cultivate the olive groves. The old centre, focused on rue St-Sauveur and place Bellevue, still has the air of a little Provençal hill village with narrow streets and a belfry with a wrought-iron campanile. Le Cannet is particularly associated with painter Pierre Bonnard, who bought a house here in 1926; staying largely remote from the social whirl of the coast below, he painted the village rooftops, the view from his window, with patches of yellow mimosa, or his beloved wife Marthe. Next to the town hall, work has started on the conversion of the Hôtel Saint-Vianney into the **Musée Bonnard** (due to open late 2009/early 2010; www.mairie-le-cannet.fr) devoted to the artist.

An ethereal mural in Le Cannet

La Californie

Later arrivals often built their villas on the hills of La Californie and Super-Cannes on the eastern side of town, still the most exclusive area to live, though fences and security gates mean that few are visible from the street. Two that can be visited are the **Chapelle Bellini** (Parc Fiorentina, 67bis avenue de Vallauris; Mon–Fri 2–5pm; free), an Italianate chapel built in 1880 that was more recently the studio of painter Emmanuel Bellini, and the **Villa Domergue** (15 avenue Fiesole; July–Sept Tue–Sun 3–7pm), the house and terraced Tuscan-style gardens designed in 1936 by society portrait painter Jean-Gabriel Domergue. After a successful career as a graphic artist for the fashion houses, Domergue, who had been taught by Toulouse-Lautrec and Degas, moved south in the 1920s, where he organised big parties, designed posters and churned out countless languid portraits of women, including Brigitte Bardot and Nadine de Rothschild. There are paintings and sculptures by Domergue and his wife around the house and garden, and the villa is used for temporary exhibitions and outdoor jazz concerts in summer. Lower down towards the sea, the neo-Gothic **Eglise Saint-Georges** (27 avenue Roi Albert) was built in 1887 in memory of Queen Victoria's youngest son, Prince Leopold, who died here in 1884. This was also the area favoured by the Russian aristocracy, as witnessed by the starry blue onion dome of the **Eglise Orthodoxe Saint-Michel Archange** (impasse des Deux Eglises, 40 boulevard Alexandre III; Sat 5–6pm).

The Iles de Lérins

A 10-minute boat ride from the Port Vieux, the **Iles de Lérins** seem a world apart from La Croisette: yet for much of its history the little fishing settlement of Cannes was merely a dependence of the monastery on Ile Saint-Honorat and the islands were frequently a prized trophy in European wars.

On board the boat to the Iles de Lérins

Ile Sainte-Marguerite

The larger of the two islands, Sainte-Marguerite is perfect for walks and picnics, and despite numerous ferries a day in summer it's still possible to get away from the crowds. There's a sheltered beach to the west of the harbour, and plenty of smaller rocky creeks to be found along the 8km (5-mile) footpath that circles the island. En route are great views of the Estérel mountain range, Ile Saint-Honorat and the Bay of Cannes. Most of the interior is covered in forest – eucalyptus, holm-oak, aleppo and parasol pines – and traversed by numerous footpaths and picnic sites. A botanical trail points out the most interesting plants, while the **Etang du Batéguier**, a small brackish lake near the western tip, is a nature reserve drawing a wide variety of birds. Look out also for a couple of *fours à boulets* – stoves used to heat up cannon balls.

Dominating the cliff on the north side of the island, a short uphill walk from the harbour is the impressive star-shaped,

Getting there

Several companies run trips from Cannes to the islands all year round, leaving from quai Laubeuf beyond the car park at the western end of the port, but note that you cannot combine both islands in one trip. Boats to Sainte-Marguerite: Horizon, tel: 04 92 98 71 36; Trans Côte d'Azur, tel: 04 92 98 71 30; to Saint-Honorat: Planaria, tel: 04 92 98 71 38.

bastioned **Royal Fort**. It was begun by Cardinal Richelieu, continued by the Spanish who occupied the island from 1635–7 during the Thirty Years War, when it made a convenient point on the way between Spain and Italy, and given its final form by Louis XIV's brilliant military engineer Vauban. Assorted buildings within the ramparts contain the long gunpowder store, the barracks and a chapel.

The old keep, which was erected in the 17th century around a medieval tower, contains the **Musée de la Marine** (June–Sept daily 10am–5.45pm, Oct–Mar Tue–Sun 10.30am–1.15pm, 2.15–4.45pm; charge), which reveals several different eras of the defence of the island. Vaulted Roman cisterns, constructed to store precious water, now contain a maquette of the original Roman *castrum*, along with fragments of mosaic and a collection of Greek amphorae found from shipwrecks that testify to an ancient wine trade. In the late 17th century, after the Revocation of the Edict of Nantes, it became one of four royal prisons in the Mediterranean where Protestants and others seen to pose a threat to the crown were held without trial. The cells contain a memorial to six Protestant priests held here, as well as a manuscript written by Scottish prisoner Andrew MacDonald, found in a hole in the wall. A series of cells are decorated with expressive modern murals by artist Jean Le Gac. The room that most stirs the imagination, however, is the cell of the Man in the Iron Mask, where the mysterious figure immortalised by Alexandre Dumas was imprisoned from 1687–98.

Ile Saint-Honorat

Smaller and wilder than Ile Sainte-Marguerite, the Ile Saint-Honorat was for centuries one of the most important religious sites in Europe, home to the powerful monastery founded around 410 by Honoratus and a small group of companions, becoming an important place of pilgrimage and a centre for evangelising the region. On a flat spit of land jutting out at the southern tip of the island is the severe **Monastère-Donjon**, which was fortified against pirate raids, with chapels and refectories set around an unusual two-tiered cloister. The remains of seven ancient chapels are dotted around the island, including the 10th-century Chapelle de la Trinité and the unusual octagonal Chapelle Saint-Caprien. During the Revolution, the monastery was confiscated as national goods and sold off to a Parisian actress who used it to host parties. In 1859, the island was acquired by the bishop of Fréjus and a new **monastery** (July–Sept daily guided visits only; www.abbayedelerins. com) was rebuilt around a medieval cloister, which now houses a small community of Cistercian monks who cultivate the vineyard and olive groves and produce a plant-based liqueur called Lérina, which you can buy in the monastery shop.

The monastery on Ile Saint-Honorat

MONACO

The second-smallest state in Europe – after the Vatican – is a tiny autocratic anomaly in the midst of republican France: a surreal place squeezed between sea and mountain, where princes and princesses and the paraphernalia of monarchy exist alongside skyscrapers and international banks that give it the air of a little Hong Kong; a tax haven for tennis players; and a jet-setters' playground, where the chief pastime is driving Ferraris around the hairpin bends. The Riviera's land pressure is at its greatest here, and Belle Epoque villas are dwarfed by apartment blocks, all straining for a sea view.

Luxury yachts compete for attention in Fontvieille harbour

Monaco divides into several distinct districts: Monte Carlo around the Casino, plus its eastward beach extension Larvotto; La Condamine around the Port Hercule; Monaco-Ville, the original town up on its rock, also known as Le Rocher; Fontvieille, on reclaimed land on the western side; and Moneghetti, inland on top of the hill. It may be just 2km (1¼ miles) square, but a one-way system and lots of tunnels make navigation complicated. Leave the car in a car park and use taxis, the efficient bus service, or go by foot – a useful system of lifts and stairways helps pedestrians to negotiate the steep hills.

Monte Carlo

Monte Carlo is the district that for most people epitomises Monaco, centred around the hub of **place du Casino**. The neatly manicured lawns and fountains of the Jardin des Boulengrins, which descend from boulevard des Moulins, make a splendid approach to the **Casino de Monte Carlo** (Mon–Fri 2pm–late, Sat–Sun noon–late; over 18s, ID required; www.casinomontecarlo.com) with its sculptures on the facade, green copper roof and twin turrets. It is hard to imagine that this was simply an olive-tree-covered hill until the 1860s, when Prince Charles III, in search of a new source of revenue following the cession of Menton and Roquebrune to France, had

Pitching up in style at the Casino de Monte Carlo

the bright idea of opening a casino. After an unenthusiastic start, the prince awarded the concession to run it to François Blanc, founder of the Société des Bains de Monaco (SBM). This company (its main shareholder is now the State of Monaco) still runs the majority of Monte Carlo's finest hotels, restaurants, casinos, spas, sporting facilities and nightclubs.

By day, tourists crowd round to take photos; by night, this is still the most glamorous of Monaco's numerous gambling establishments, where roulette and blackjack are played against a backdrop of allegorical paintings and chandeliers. There's a separate entrance for the *salons privés*, reserved for high-staking players. In 1878, Blanc's widow Marie called in architect Charles Garnier, who had recently designed the Paris Opera, to add an opera house to encourage gamblers to stay in town a little longer. The **Salle Garnier** was inaugurated in January 1879, tacked on the back of the casino. Over the years the opera has welcomed renowned singers, from Adelina Patty, Nelly Melba and Russian Schaliapine to Plácido Domingo, as well as becoming home to Diaghilev's Ballets Russes. The auditorium is a gorgeous confection, painstakingly restored in 2005 right down to five different shades of gold leaf. Opera and casino share the same foyer, giving a unique opportunity for a flutter in the interval.

Around the Casino

On one side of the casino, historic brasserie **Café de Paris** has a superb terrace for watching the comings and goings on the square; inside, slot machines are busy all day long, while the renovated gaming tables have a Formula 1 theme. Across the square, Rolls-Royces and Ferraris line up outside the **Hôtel de Paris**, built by the SBM in 1864, the first and still grandest of the grand hotels, with the Louis XV restaurant and the Bar Américain. In the splendid lobby, the horse's knee on the equestrian statue of Louis XIV has been polished gold by superstitious gamblers hoping for good luck.

This is also Monaco's smartest shopping territory, with jewellers and designer labels lining avenue des Beaux-Arts and place Beaumarchais between the Hôtel de Paris and the huge Belle Epoque **Hôtel Hermitage** (which now has a putting green on the roof).

Below the Casino gardens, a lift and stairs descend to the roof terraces of the huge Spelugues complex (the original name of the district before Prince Charles renamed it after himself) built in 1978. Constructed like a series of

As seen on screen

The Casino de Monte Carlo is a favourite movie location. It features in Hitchcock's *Rebecca* and his Riviera romp *To Catch a Thief*, with Grace Kelly and Cary Grant, in Jacques Demy's *La Baie des Anges* and Victor Saville's *24 Hours of a Woman's Life*. Another casino habitué is James Bond, who tries his luck in both *GoldenEye* and *Never Say Never Again*.

overlapping hexagons jutting out on concrete stilts into the water over a roaring road tunnel, it comprises the 616-room Fairmont Hotel, apartments and the **Auditorium Rainier III** congress centre, which has a mosaic on the roof by Op artist Victor Vasarely. On its fringes, operations are under way for the construction of Le Portier, 12 hectares (30 acres) of accommodation and office space set to be claimed from the sea.

Further East

In a garden on avenue Princesse Grace, the peach-and-cream stucco Villa Stauber contains the **Musée National des Poupées et des Automates** (daily 10am–6.30pm; charge; www.nmnm.mc), the national museum of the miniature-sized state, devoted to dolls. The old-fashioned collection focuses on elegantly attired 19th-century porcelain figures,

Monaco Grand Prix

Held around the narrow streets of Monte Carlo and La Condamine, the Monaco Grand Prix is considered the slowest but most difficult of the Formula I races, with its notorious chicane bends, changes of level and road-tunnel exit. The first race was organised on 14 April 1929 by the Automobile Club de Monaco and won by a certain William Grover-Williams in a green Bugatti, and it became part of the new Formula I season in the 1950s. Since then Ayrton Senna won it six times, Graham Hill and Michael Schumacher five times each. People reserve tickets for the grandstands along the Port Hercule or in race-side hotels, restaurants and apartment roof terraces months, even years, ahead, champagne lunches included, or watch from private yachts in the harbour. Once the grandstands and barriers have been dismantled, the roads are returned to the Bentleys, Ferraris and Lamborghinis that generally occupy them, though various companies offer tourists the chance of experiencing at least a semblance of the thrills in a red Ferrari.

along with the miniature dinner services, rosewood furniture and copper jelly moulds suited to their station. Highlights of the museum are the fragile vintage automatons, which are set in motion several times a day.

Over the street, the **Japanese Garden** (daily 9am–sunset) on the quayside provides a touch of oriental Zen calm, with streams traversed by stepping stones and Japanese

Monaco's man-made
Larvotto Beach

bridges, Shinto shrines, raked gravel and trees trimmed into sculptural forms. Behind it, the polygonal glass-and-copper structure overlooking the sea is just the tip of the iceberg that is **Grimaldi Forum** (July–Aug Mon–Sat 10am–8pm, Sept–June noon–7pm; charge; www.grimaldiforum. com): a huge, partially buried venue for art exhibitions, congresses, concerts and occasional ballet and opera productions, as well as the Zebra Square restaurant and Kare(ment) nightclub.

Beyond here Monaco's man-made **Larvotto Beach** is mostly public, with coarse imported sand and a couple of restaurants, bordered to the east by the Méridien Beach Plaza and the Sporting Club d'Eté, opened in the 1970s, home to restaurants and Monaco's most famous nightclub, Jimmy'z.

La Condamine

The natural deep-water harbour of the **Port Hercule** has been used ever since the Greek Phocaean trading post of Monoikos. Today the port is one of the prime spots for the Formula 1 Grand Prix, when grandstands are set up along

The view over Port Hercule from Monaco-Ville

quai Albert I. The rest of the year, with its large outdoor swimming pool (transformed into an ice rink in winter) and pizzerias, it is used for all sorts of events, ranging from international showjumping in June to a water splash and funfair in August. Quai Antoine I is home to the ever-fashionable American restaurant Stars 'n' Bars, while the spectacle of swanky yachts with multi-storey decks and uniformed crews makes **quai des Etats-Unis** a favourite promenade. The port has grown since 2000, with the construction of a counter-jetty, designed to keep out easterly winds and welcome in the yachts of the ultra-rich, and a massive semi-floating concrete dyke towed across from Spain to accommodate vast cruise ships.

Alongside the port, now squeezed under a flyover, the **Eglise Sainte-Dévote** (daily 8.30am–6pm) is dedicated to the principality's patron saint, Corsican Saint Devota, who is said to have drifted ashore here in the 4th century. The church, begun in the 11th century, was almost entirely re-constructed in the 19th. A boat is burnt on the cobbled square in front each 26 January on the eve of the saint's feast.

Inland, mainly low-rise **La Condamine** is about as close as Monaco gets to everyday living, with a few Belle Epoque terraces and the lively restaurant-lined rue Princesse Caroline.

Under the shadow of Le Rocher, arcaded **place des Armes** is home to a **covered food market** (mornings daily) with quirky bars and stalls inside selling meat, patisserie and pasta – each with a photo of the current prince proudly on display – and fruit and vegetable stalls outside on the square.

Monaco-Ville

Sitting on top of its rock, Le Rocher or Monaco-Ville is dominated by the picturebook Palais Princier on place du Palais, still the royal residence, ruled – apart from a few interludes – by the Grimaldi family ever since François Grimaldi sneaked in disguised as a monk in 1297. Walk up from place des Armes or take one of the frequent buses, which deposit you on place de la Visitation, a 10-minute walk from place du Palais. The square lined with cannons and pyramids of cannon balls provides great views from the ramparts on each side. Each day, the changing of the guard takes place promptly at 11.55am, accompanied by much marching and drum-beating.

The **Palais Princier** (daily Apr 10.30am–6pm, May–Sept 9.30am–6.30pm, Oct 10am–5.30pm; charge; www.palais.mc) was constructed around the fortress begun by the Genoans in the 13th century and embellished during the Renaissance when the frescoed, arcaded Galerie d'Hercule overlooking the Cour d'Honneur was built, with a double horseshoe staircase modelled on Fontainebleau. The excellent audio guide (complete with a welcome from the prince) included with the ticket moves through the State Apartments, taking in the

On parade at the Palais Princier

mirror gallery, the bright-blue Louis XV room, panelled Mazarin room and the bedroom where Edward Augustus, duke of York and brother of George III, died in 1767 after falling ill en route for Genoa; and finishes in the Throne Room, with a fireplace in La Turbie marble and a canopied Empire-style throne where Prince Albert II was crowned in 2005, all accompanied by an awful lot of royal portraits.

Exploring the Old Town

An adjacent doorway to the State Apartments leads to the **Musée des Souvenirs Napoléoniens et Collection des Archives Historiques du Palais** (daily Apr 10.30am–6pm, May–Sept 9.30am–6.30pm, Oct 10am–5.30pm, Dec–Mar 10.30am–5pm; charge; www.palais.mc), an eclectic array of Napoleonic memorabilia amassed by Prince Louis II, a descendant of the emperor's adopted daughter Stéphanie de Beauharnais. Among exhibits are a bust by Canova, an ornate cradle and the black hat worn by Napoleon when in exile on Elba. On the mezzanine above is a collection of medals and archive documents relating to Monaco's history.

The Old Town's handful of narrow streets of pastel-coloured houses, now largely taken up by souvenir shops, make an intriguingly folksy contrast to Monte Carlo. Bypassed by most visitors is the **Chapelle de la Miséricorde** (daily 10am–6pm; free) with striped marble walls, white marble sculptures and a painted wooden sculpture of the *Dead Christ* attributed to Monaco-born François-Joseph Bosio (1768–1845), which is paraded through the town on Good Friday. Also worth visiting is the pretty 17th-century **Chapelle de la Visitation** (Tue–Sun 10am–4pm; charge), which provides an appropriate setting for a fine private collection of Baroque religious art that includes paintings of saints Peter and Paul by Rubens, works by Ribera and Zurbarán, and a set of Spanish grisaille paintings.

Monaco-Ville's neo-Romanesque cathedral

Cathedral and Aquarium

The **Cathédrale** (daily 8am–6pm, closed during services) was built in 1875 and is a severe neo-Romanesque affair, with flags along the nave and a Byzantine-style mosaic over the altar, made by the same craftsmen who worked on the Casino. In the side chapels are reliquaries of Saint Devota, Monaco's patron saint, and of Roman legionary Saint Roman, and an altarpiece by Ludovico Bréa showing St Nicolas surrounded by saints, among them Saint Devota. The simple slab-like tombs of the princes of Monaco are set into the ground around the apse, drawing visitors and pilgrims especially to those of Princess Grace, who was laid to rest in 1982 *(see page 73)*, and Prince Rainier, who joined her here in 2005.

In an imposing white building that descends down the cliff face from avenue St-Martin, the extremely popular **Musée Océanographique et Aquarium** (Apr–June and Sept daily 9.30am–7pm, July–Aug 9.30am–7.30pm, Oct–Mar 10am–

Fountain fun in Monaco

6pm; charge; www.oceano.mc) was founded in 1910 by sea-faring Prince Albert I, 'the scientist prince', who trained in the French navy before setting off on countless oceano-graphic expeditions, mostly to the Arctic. The upstairs museum is an elegant time-warp tribute to his voyages, with its wooden cases, whale skeletons, navigation charts, and glass jars containing preserved specimens. The chief attraction is the downstairs aquarium, where cleverly lit tanks, fed by water pumped in directly from the sea, include a shark pit and living coral reefs populated by brightly coloured species from the Mediterranean and tropical oceans.

In the gardens that descend below avenue de la Porte Neuve, the ruined 18th-century **Fort Saint-Antoine** on the headland is now an amphitheatre used in summer for out-door performances, while lower down by the Parking des Pêcheurs car park is the **Cinéma d'Eté**, where recently re-leased movies are screened outdoors in the summer months.

Fontvieille

This entire new district, created on 25 hectares (60 acres) of land reclaimed from the sea, was one of the pharaonic projects of the 1960s that earned Rainier III the label 'the builder prince' – a vast complex of bland apartment blocks in neo-Provençal tones around a yachting marina, with a number of bars and brasseries popular with international expats. West of the marina bordering Cap d'Ail lie the heliport, the **Stade Louis II** (3 avenue des Castelans), home to Monaco football club, which plays in the French premier league, along with an athletics track and an Olympic-size swimming pool; the Espace Châpiteau, a permanent big top used for the prestigious circus festival each January; and the **Princesse Grace rose garden** (daily 8am–sunset; free), where 4,000 rose bushes have been planted in a heart-shaped design, in memory of the princess who died under what are still mysterious circumstances in a car accident on the Corniche in 1982.

Local people, however, come to Fontvieille for the shopping centre, with a big Carrefour hypermarket. From here, escalators climb to **Terrasses de Fontvieille**, a rather bizarre setting for a cluster of small museums.

Homage to Grace

The parcours Princesse Grace is a trail of 25 places in the principality that are associated with the former Hollywood film star Grace Kelly, who married Prince Rainier III in 1956. Sites are marked by panels with black-and-white press photos of the princess carrying out royal functions.

A Trio of Museums

The **Musée des Timbres et des Monnaies** (daily July–Sept 9.30am–6pm, Oct–June 9.30am–5pm; charge; www.oetp-monaco.com), with a stamp shop on site, is devoted to Monaco stamps (since 1885) and coins (since 1641), which are popular with philatelists and numismatists. The **Musée Naval** (daily 10am–6pm; charge; www.musee-naval.mc) houses ship models tracing maritime history.

Not surprisingly in motor-racing-crazy Monaco, the most substantial member of the group is the **Collection de Voitures Anciennes de SAS le Prince de Monaco** (daily 10am–6pm; charge; www.palais.mc), the collection of vintage cars amassed by Prince Rainier III. They range from a Dion Bouton made in 1903 and an early Panhard et Levassor from 1907 via lots of vintage Rolls-Royces and Princess Grace's humbler Renault Floride to modern racing cars, including Nigel Mansell's Formula 1 Ferrari, as well as some utilitarian vehicles from the Monaco fire brigade and some early horse-drawn carriages.

A recent addition is a prototype racing car ALA50 manufactured in Monaco by Monte Carlo Automobile and given to Prince Albert II for his 50th birthday in 2008.

A Jardin Exotique cactus flower

To the side of the museum is a small zoo, the **Jardin Animalier** (daily June–Sept 9am–noon, 2–7pm, Oct–Feb 10am–noon, 2–5pm, Mar–May 10am–noon, 2–6pm; charge), founded by Prince Rainier. Among its creatures are monkeys, a hippo, a rare white tiger and exotic birds.

Moneghetti

Monaco's last attraction on the way out of town towards Nice is probably its best. The **Jardin Exotique** (62 boulevard du Jardin Exotique; daily mid-May–mid-Sept 9am–7pm, mid-Sept–mid-May 9am–6pm; charge; www.jardin-exotique. mc), opened in 1933, is a fantasy land of cactuses and succulents, among them giant agaves, whole colonies of grandmother's pincushions and 11-metre (36ft) high euphorbes, some of them over a century old, planted in steep terraces and gulleys down the cliff. The entrance ticket also includes the **Grotto de l'Observatoire** (guided visits only) at the foot of the garden, a deep limestone cave full of stalactites and stalagmites, and the rather dry **Musée d'Anthropologie Préhistorique**, displaying archaeological finds, mainly from the Grimaldi caves just across the Italian border.

The Jardin Exotique provides panoramic views over Monaco

From late 2009, the 1920s Villa Paloma nearby is temporary home to the **Nouveau Musée National de Monaco** (www.nmnm.mc). Temporary exhibitions and a floor devoted to Dutch artist Kees van Dongen are intended to give a foretaste of the future national art museum. The new museum, which is projected to open in 2015, will be the subject of an architectural competition, but its site has yet to be found, or reclaimed from the sea.

EXCURSIONS

Cagnes-sur-Mer

Just 13km (8 miles) west of Nice, Cagnes-sur-Mer is a popular excursion for the Niçois for a meal out in the medieval
hill village of Haut-de-Cagnes, Renoir's house at Les Collettes, the Hippodrome racecourse and a 3.5km (2-mile)
shingle beach. At the top of picturesque Haut-de-Cagnes,
with its steep, winding streets of creeper-covered houses,
many now containing restaurants and galleries, is the
Château Musée Grimaldi (Wed–Mon May–Sept 10am–
noon, 2–6pm, Oct–Apr until 5pm; charge). This was a
watchtower constructed by one of the branches of the
Grimaldi family, before being converted into a sumptuous
Renaissance residence. A galleried, vaulted loggia leads to

Matisse's Chapel

During World War II the elderly Matisse retreated to Vence (14km/9 miles
from Cagnes-sur-Mer) to avoid the bombing, renting Villa Le Rêve, where
young Monique Bourgeois (later Sister Jacques Marie) nursed and sat for
him. In gratitude he offered to decorate the Chapelle du Rosaire for the
Dominican order, and ended up designing everything from the building itself with its blue-and-white glazed pantiles to the priest's cope and the
gilded crucifix that stands on the altar. The **Chapelle du Rosaire-Henri
Matisse** (route de St-Jeannet, Vence; Mon–Sat 2–5.30pm, Tue, Thur also
10–11.30am; charge) is a meeting of Matisse's mastery of line in the pared-
back drawings of *St Dominic*, the *Virgin and Child* and *Stations of the Cross*
in black on white tiles, and of colour in the stained glass, whose reflections
send dapples of blue, yellow and green across the walls. Too ill to attend
the opening ceremony, Matisse nonetheless sent along a text: 'This work
took four years of assiduous work and is the summary of all my active life.
I consider it, despite all its imperfections, as my masterpiece.'

a magnificent ceremonial chamber, with carved fireplace and dramatic 1620 *trompe l'œil* ceiling with the *Fall of Phaethon*, attributed to Genoese painter Giulio Benso Pietra. The château also contains a small display devoted to olives, the municipal art collection and the surprising Collection Suzy Solidor, donated by the Montparnasse cabaret singer who was painted by many of the successful portaitists of the 1920s. This gives the unusual opportunity of seeing

Detail from the Chapelle du Rosaire-Henri Matisse

the same person depicted by Kisling, Foujita, Van Dongen, Cocteau and Tamara de Lempicka.

The Musée Renoir

Down the hill, east of the modern centre of Cagnes-sur-Mer, the Domaine Les Collettes, now the **Musée Renoir** (Dec–mid-Nov Wed–Mon 10am–noon, 2–5pm, May–Sept until 6pm; charge), was bought by the elderly Renoir in 1908. Although now surrounded by urban sprawl and apartment blocks that have partly obscured the view, the house and gardens have changed little since Renoir lived here, receiving visitors such as Pierre Bonnard and Matisse, who painted the garden, as well as photographer Willy Maywald, whose photos hang on the stairs.

Paintings around the house include a study for the large *Late Bathers*, its heightened, almost garish, palette no doubt something to do with the Riviera's bright sunshine, which

Renoir described as 'maddening'; and a charming small portrait of his youngest son Claude, *Coco Reading*, dressed in a sailor suit that can still be seen hanging in the studio. But Renoir, almost crippled by arthritis, increasingly turned to sculpture, producing small bronzes in collaboration with his assistant Richard Guino (who is credited as co-author) and later with Louis Morel.

Mougins

Just 8km (5 miles) inland from Cannes, the chic little hill village of Mougins is a lively gastronomic night out from town, with some of the best restaurants in the region and a foodie festival each September. On the main square, **place Lamy**, art galleries, craft shops and a clutter of gourmet bistros surround a fountain with a rusty statue of 19th-century explorer General Lamy, born in the town. Above here pristine stepped *ruelles* wind up to the much-altered Romanesque church with its wrought-iron campanile. Round the corner by the Porte Sarrazine, a fortified 15th-century gateway, the **Musée de la Photographie** (Mon–Fri 10am–6pm, Sat–Sun 11am–6pm; free) has a collection of early cameras and a fascinating array of portraits of Picasso by Doisneau, Lartigue, Clergue, Villers and others, as well as temporary exhibitions.

The church at Mougins

Outside the old village, near Picasso's former villa and the 17th-century chapel of Notre-Dame de Vie, is Mougins's biggest gastronomic destination, the Moulin des Mougins – a converted oil mill now run by hot young chef Alain Llorca.

The TGV follows the distinctive Corniche d'Or coastal route

The Estérel

The Estérel massif offers the most astonishing colours on the Riviera and can be travelled in an easy loop from Cannes by coastal N98 one way and A8 or N7 the other. Unlike the arid white limestone of the Alpes-Maritimes, here the rock is deep-red porphyry, which contrasts with the Mediterranean blue, with parasol pines, garrigue scrub and the yellow of mimosa in winter. The initial section of coast road nearest to Cannes is highly built up as it passes through La Napoule and Théoule-sur-Mer, but later the scenery becomes more natural. For centuries this was a wild, inaccessible area, terrorised by 18th-century bandit Gaspard de Bresse, a sort of French Robin Hood, from his base at Les Adrets de l'Estérel (now the wrong side of the N7), and the Corniche d'Or road (N98) was constructed by the Touring Club de France only in 1903.

On the shore at La Napoule, 8km (5 miles) west of Cannes, the **Château de la Napoule** (gardens daily 10am–6pm;

Shopping in atmospheric
Fréjus Old Town

guided visits of château June–Sept daily 11.30am, 2.30pm, 3.30pm, 4.30pm; rest of year times vary; charge; www.chateau-lanapoule.com) is a too-good-to-be-true medieval castle fancifully restored in the 1920s by eccentric American sculptor Henry Clews, who added extra turrets, a gatehouse and ramparts. Clews, a scion of a New York banking family, and his wife Marie dressed in period attire and peppered the castle and topiaried gardens with moral mottoes and Henry's strange sculptures and gargoyles.

Beyond Théoule-sur-Mer, footpaths lead to the unspoilt **Pointe de l'Aiguille** headland, while at the little harbour of **La Figuierette** several footpaths and forestry tracks head into the interior, climbing to the Pic de l'Ours or to the Col Notre-Dame, where a 12-metre (40ft) high modern statue of Notre-Dame d'Afrique gazes across the sea to a similar statue in Algeria. Further west, past Trayas and Cap Roux, the gorgeous creek of **Agay** is a family resort, with a touch of nostalgia for its 1930s heyday. Just off the coast, the Ile d'Or served as model for Hergé's *Tintin et l'Ile Noire*. The nearby Plage du Dramont was one of the main landing beaches for Allied troops from North Africa in the 1944 liberation of Provence.

At the western edge of the massif, **Saint-Raphaël** is a low-key resort focused around its yachting marina and palm-lined seafront, no longer the fashionable destination it was in the late 19th century. More interesting is adjoining **Fréjus**, once the important Roman port of Forum Julii. There's an impressive ruined amphitheatre, now used for bullfighting and concerts, and fragments of the Roman aqueduct on the outskirts, but the gem is the **cathedral complex** (June–Sept daily 9am–6.30pm, Oct–May Tue–Sun 9am–noon, 2–5pm; charge) in the centre of the Old Town. Anyone can visit the cathedral, but you should take one of the frequent guided tours to see the 5th-century baptistery, the cloister with an unusual wooden ceiling decorated with animals and mythical beasts, and the cathedral's elaborately carved doors.

Venturing Inland

Inland from the coast, the climate changes and the scenery becomes more Alpine. By car from Cannes the Route Napoléon (N85) roughly follows the mountain route taken by Napoleon on his march on Paris after escaping from Elba in 1815. After the perfume town of **Grasse**, the route becomes more grandiose, with views of snow-topped peaks in the distance, crossing St-Vallier-de-Thiey on the stony Plateau de Caussols and forested Escragnolles, before arriving at pretty **Castellane**, known for its strange fossils and perched under a rocky outcrop at the entrance to the spectacular Gorges de Verdon; it then continues to the dignified spa town of **Digne-les-Bains**, and on northwards via fortified Sisteron to Gap. An alternative is to take the **Train des Pignes** (www.trainprovence.com), a scenic narrow-gauge railway between the Gare de Provence in Nice and Digne. Stops include Puget-Théniers, **Entrevaux**, with an imposing citadel high above the River Var, and picturesque **Annot**. Vintage steam trains run between Puget-Théniers and Entrevaux some Sundays in summer (reserve on tel: 04 97 03 80 80).

WHAT TO DO

Beyond sightseeing and eating out, there are plenty of things to keep the visitor occupied. All three cities offer endless shopping and window-shopping opportunities. In summer, the beach and water sports are the obvious choice for activities, complemented by a host of outdoor music festivals and fireworks displays. The rest of the year the busy agenda ranges from Nice's traditional Carnaval and the Monte Carlo Car Rally to opera and ballet.

SHOPPING

What to Buy Where

Nice, Cannes and Monaco are all major shopping destinations. Cosmopolitan Nice offers the greatest variety, while Cannes and Monaco are firmly targeted at the luxury fashion market, with an adventurous, trendy edge in Cannes and more conservative styles in Monaco.

In Nice, smart designer labels are concentrated along avenue de Suède, avenue de Verdun, rue Paradis and rue Alphonse Karr, where you'll find Chanel, Emporio Armani, Cartier, Max Mara and Kenzo as well as the 'preppy' men's and women's wear of Nice-based Façonnable. Among more unusual shops, **Désert** at 9 rue Alphonse Karr is hot on the latest trends from designers such as Marc Jacobs, Isabel Marrant and Tsumori Chisato; **Espace Harroch** on rue Paradis is a chic multi-level, multi-label outlet for men's and women's clothes, kitchenware and interior design items.

For more mainstream chain stores, go to Rue de France, rue Masséna and avenue Jean Médecin, home to practical

The Côte d'Azur is a windsurfer's paradise

supermarket **Monoprix**, **Fnac** book, music, photo and computer superstore and the **Centre Etoile** shopping centre.

In Vieux Nice, food shops and souvenir outlets mix with art and craft galleries and New Agey clothes shops, such as **Fashion Gallery** (rue St-Suaire), and organic and ethical clothing outlet **L'Ile aux Fées** (8 rue Benoît Bunico). **Village Ségurane** is an arcade of 40 antiques dealers on rue Ségurane between place Garibaldi and the Vieux Port.

In Cannes, high-end boutiques are concentrated along La Croisette, rue d'Antibes and the **Gray d'Albion** mall that runs between the two. For diamond necklaces and haute couture dresses suitable for walking up *les marches*, the most prestigious labels (Lacroix, Cartier, Balenciaga, Ferragamo) cluster on La Croisette, with younger styles, such as Paul & Joe, Zadig & Voltaire and Italian labels Missoni and Patricia Pepe on rue d'Antibes. Rue Meynadier near the food market is lined with outlets for cheaper casual wear and beach gear.

Monaco's 'golden rectangle' is on place du Casino and avenue des Beaux-Arts, which conveniently stretches between the Hôtel de Paris and Hôtel Hermitage. **Galerie du Métropole** is an upmarket mall, next to Hôtel Métropole; more

Jewellery for sale in Monaco

boutiques can be found amid luxury car dealers on avenue Princesse Grace and boulevard des Moulins. Up in Monaco-Ville, the **Chocolaterie de Monaco** is a rare exception to the many souvenir shops. Monégasques go to Fontvieille just for the huge Centre Commercial, home to Carrefour hypermarket, clothing chains and the sports equipment store Decathlon.

Food and Wine

As in any French town, the food market is an essential part of life, and **cours Saleya** market in Vieux Nice, the **Marché Forville** in Cannes and the **Marché de la Condamine** in Monaco are the places for stocking up on fresh produce for a picnic and for observing local life.

Good items to take home include olive oil and related products such as table olives, tapenades, soaps and olive-wood bowls. French olive oil production is tiny by Italian and Spanish standards, but it is usually of high quality. The Nice area has an *appellation d'origine contrôlée* (AOC) for

Cannes's Marché Forville

oil made from its tiny purple *cailletier* olive. Outlets include **Alviari** on rue St-François-de-Paule, which presses oil at its own mill, and **Oliviera** on rue du Collet (both in Vieux Nice), and stalls in Cannes's Marché Forville; the flavour varies from producer to producer, and you can usually taste before buying.

Look out also for chocolates, candied fruit and other gourmet items from **Maison Auer**, truffles at **Terres de Truffes**, both in Vieux Nice, home-made pasta from **Maison Barale** in Vieux Nice and Marché de la Condamine. Other regional produce includes wines from Bellet *(see page 104)* and the Lérina liqueur made by the monks on Ile Saint-Honorat *(see page 61)*. The oldest wine shop in Nice is **Cave Bianchi** on rue Raoul Bosio, which also has a branch in Cannes.

ARTS AND ENTERTAINMENT

Performing Arts

While the south of France is often remembered for its summer festivals, both Nice and Monaco have an active year-round arts calendar. In fact, the serious arts season runs from September or October to June; over July and August the performing arts tend to move outdoors, with theatre productions in the Fort Saint-Antoine in Monaco, Nice's renowned jazz festival in Cimiez, *La Castillada* – a *promenade-spectacle* on the castle hill – and electronic music and chamber music events in Cannes. For information, look out for the *Saison des Cultures* booklet published by the Mairie de Nice and the culture agenda on www.nice.fr; the brochures *Sortir à Cannes* (Oct–Apr) and *L'Eté à Cannes* (May–Sept); and the publication *La Semaine des Spectacles* available at news-stands.

Carnaval de Nice

For the two weeks leading up to Shrove Tuesday, Nice lets its hair down in the annual Carnaval, a pre-Lenten tradition going back to the Middle Ages – and probably to pagan festivals before. It took its present form in the late 19th century when the municipality organised what had been a raucous event of street dancing and masked balls into a parade of carnival floats. Today, there's a different theme each year (king of masquerades in 2009) as colourfully decorated floats, dancers, musicians and giant carnival figures with papier mâché heads parade noisily each night behind the King of Carnaval, culminating with fireworks on the last night. In the afternoon, thousands of flowers are thrown in the *bataille des fleurs* along the promenade des Anglais. You have to pay for reserved seats along the promenade des Anglais, but you can join the crowds around the Jardins Albert 1 for free (www.nicecarnaval.com).

The **Opéra de Monte Carlo** (www.opera.mc) offers a glamorous night out amid the gilt and chandeliers of the opera house adjoining the casino. Under director-choreographer Jean-Christophe Maillot **Ballets de Monte Carlo**, the descendant of Diaghilev's Ballets Russes, has become one of Europe's top troupes. It generally performs in the Grimaldi Forum when not on tour, as do some large-scale visiting operatic productions. First-

Carnaval mask

rate contemporary international dance companies take part in the biennial **Cannes Dance Festival** in December. The **Opéra de Nice** (www.opera-nice.org) is another fine opera house, with a plush crimson-and-gold interior. It stages a wide range of productions, along with ballet and classical concerts by the respected **Orchestra Philharmonique**. Nice is also home to the **Ensemble Baroque de Nice**, one of France's leading early-music ensembles, and the experimental contemporary music institute CIRM, which organises the **MANCA** festival (www.cirm-manca.org) in November. The **Théâtre National de Nice** (www.tnn.fr), on the promenade des Arts, is the most important of several in Nice, especially for new drama. In Cannes, most events take place in the **Palais des Festivals** (www.palaisdesfestivals.com).

Rock and Jazz
Big-name rock bands and French *variété* singers peform at the vast **Palais Nikaia** (www.nikaia.fr) and **Acropolis Congress**

Centre (www.nice-acropolis.com) in Nice and in the **Grimaldi Forum** in Monaco; **Théâtre Lino Ventura** is a recently opened venue in Nice with a programme of pop music and contemporary dance; local bands and British indie groups turn up at popular **Wayne's Bar** in the Old Town. In summer, there are outdoor concerts in the **Théâtre de Verdure** in the Jardin Albert I. The **Monte Carlo Sporting Festival** at the Sporting d'Eté features young pop divas along with rock and soul legends, while recently opened **Moods** (www.montecarloresort. com), located under the Café de Paris in Monte Carlo, is a music bar with rock, jazz and blues.

Nice Jazz Festival (www.nicejazzfestival.fr) in July has a relaxed atmosphere as spectators wander between three stages in the Roman arena and gardens by the Matisse Museum in Cimiez. It encompasses a wide spectrum of music, ranging from celebrated jazz veterans to soul, blues, funk, folk and hip hop.

Alfresco drinks in Monte Carlo

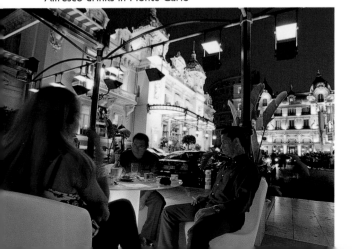

NIGHTLIFE

Cannes offers plenty of sophisticated nightlife. During the film festival, trendy Paris clubs come south and stage parties, and **Jimmy'z** opens in the Palais des Festivals. In July and August, **Le Palais** in the Palais des Festivals hosts international DJs, as does Hôtel Martinez's chic **Z Plage**, while the **Pantiero** festival focuses on new electronic music trends.

The rest of the year, the hub of trendy lounge bars with DJs is a block back from La Croisette on rue du Docteur Monod and rue des Frères Pratignac, led by **Loft** and its sister restaurant **Tantra**, **4U** and recent Italian arrival **Via Notte**. Other regulars include gay bar **Vogue** on rue du Suquet, weekend DJ parties at **Hôtel 3.14** and the **Palm Club** at the Palm Beach Casino. Classy all-night restaurant, sushi bar and discotheque **Baoli** on Port Pierre Canto draws a VIP crowd and has a tough door-selection policy.

Nice is curiously short on top club venues. Here nightlife revolves more around an active pub scene, and lounge bars serving finger food. Stalwarts include the longstanding gay **Le Klub** (6 rue Halévy), the Latino **La Bodeguita del Havana** (14 rue Chauvain), serving salsa music and South American food in a metal-framed building designed by Gustave Eiffel, and DJ and cocktail bar the **Ghost House** (3 rue de la Barillerie).

Clubbing in Monaco is generally for the affluent. **Jimmy'z** at the Sporting d'Eté is where you'll find the Monaco princesses, racing drivers, rock stars and top models along with sugar daddies and the new Eastern European millionaires, but the best clubbing in town is at **Kare(ment)** in the Grimaldi Forum. There's a more laid-back mood with DJs and live bands at **La Rascasse** and **Stars 'n' Bars** *(see page 141)* by the Port Hercule, and a more traditional piano bar ambience at the **Living Room** on avenue de Spélugues.

Casinos

The sumptuous **Casino de Monte Carlo** is the most beautiful and famous of Monte Carlo's assorted casinos, but other options include the **Casino Café de Paris**, where punters crowd the slot machines from 10am until the early hours (table games from 8pm); fairground-themed **Sun Casino** inside the Fairmont Hotel, which has an emphasis on 'American games' (American roulette, poker, blackjack, craps), while the **Monte Carlo Bay Casino** has high-tech slot machines only. Smart dress is required for the **Summer Casino** at the Sporting d'Eté, and none of Monte Carlo's casinos allow in priests, or soldiers in uniform (www.montecarlocasinos.com).

The Casino de Monte Carlo is the ultimate in glamour

At Cannes, there are three casinos: **Casino Croisette** (www.lucienbarriere.com), in the Palais des Festivals, **Les Princes** (www.lucienbarriere.com), in the Palais Stéphanie Hotel, and the **Palm Beach Casino** (www.lepalmbeach.com) at Pointe Croisette, a legendary 1930s venue that reopened in 2002. Nice has two casinos on the promenade des Anglais: at No. 1, glitzy 1970s-style **Casino Ruhl** (www.lucienbarriere.com), with slot machines, gaming tables and a Vegas-style revue (weekends except July and Aug); and the revived neo-Art Deco **Palais de la Méditerranée** (No.13).

SPORTS AND ACTIVITIES

Beaches and Swimming

Private beach concessions provide sun loungers, parasols and changing rooms; some have water-sports facilities and many have restaurants serving excellent food, from classic grilled fish and salads to cosmopolitan modern cuisine. Others morph into cocktail and DJ bars in the evening, while a few provide beauty treatments and massages. In Nice, the long pebble beach has plenty of public areas, with showers and loos, between the private concessions. In Cannes, if you're not paying for a private beach along La Croisette, head to the mainly public **Plage du Mourré Rouge** to the east or **Plage du Midi** to the west. Monaco's **Larvotto Beach** is surprisingly small. You may want to cross the frontier to the unspoilt **Plage Cabbé** at Roquebrune Cap-Martin to the east, where there's also bathing off the rocks from the Sentier du Littoral coast path, or west to Cap d'Ail, where, if you're prepared for a walk down the steps, lovely **Plage Mala** has a spectacular setting in a small bay with mountains descending straight to the sea. Note that topless bathing has gone out of fashion – you won't see many people in monokinis now.

Bat and ball on the beach

Sailing and Water Sports

Jet skis, parascending, pedalos and water-skiing are available at several of Cannes's and Nice's private beaches. For dinghy sailing classes and hire, try: **L'Aigle Nautique**, 50 boulevard Franck Pilatte, Nice; tel: 04 93 56 77 99, a water-sports centre that is

The Monaco Grand Prix

home to assorted sailing, sea-kayaking, rowing and diving clubs and schools, on the eastern edge of the Vieux Port.

Diving
The shipwrecks, underwater caves and marine fauna and flora of the Alpes-Maritimes offer some spectacular diving. Try: **L'Aigle Nautique**, Nice *(see previous page)*; **Aqua Evolution**, Pointe Croisette, Cannes; tel: 04 93 43 40 42; www.aqua-evolution.fr, for deep-sea diving courses and expeditions, sea-kayaking classes and equipment hire; or **Cannes Plongée Club**, quai St-Pierre, Cannes; tel: 04 93 38 67 57, which offers diving around the Iles de Lérins.

Golf
The Riviera has some of France's best golf courses. **Royal Mougins Golf Club**, 424 avenue du Roi, Mougins; tel: 04 92 92 49 69; www.royalmougins.fr has an 18-hole course, plus

spa and hotel, just outside Cannes. **Monte Carlo Golf Club La Turbie**, tel: 04 92 41 50 70, is an 18-hole course in a spectacular 900-metre (2,950ft) setting on Mont Agel. Also check www.rivieragolfer.com.

Gyms and Fitness

Many of the upmarket hotels have small gyms and fitness rooms. For a more serious workout and a wide range of exercise classes try **Fitness Land** (www.fitnessland.fr), with two branches in Nice, and the associated **Espace Wellness**, which also has aqua-gym sessions.

Skiing

Nice residents like to boast that they can be on the ski slopes in the morning and on the beach in the afternoon. The nearest ski stations to Nice are **Valberg**, **Auron** and **Isola 2000** in the Mercantour; from Cannes it is easier to reach **Gréolières Les Neiges** on the Massif du Cheiron.

Tennis and Squash

Monte Carlo Country Club, 155 avenue Princesse Grace, Roquebrune-Cap Martin; tel: 04 93 41 72 00; www.mccc.mc is a luxury club with clay tennis courts, squash, pool and gym. Day membership available. The following have courts which can be hired by the hour: **Nice Lawn Tennis Club**, 5 avenue Suzanne Lenglen, Nice; tel: 04 92 15 58 00; www.niceltc.com, a century-old private club with lawn and clay courts; **Tennis-Squash Club Vauban**, 18 rue Maréchal Vauban, Nice; tel: 04 93 26 09 78; **Tennis Club de Cannes**, 11 rue Lacour, Cannes; tel: 04 93 43 58 85; www.tennis-cannes.com.

Spectator Sports

The Riviera's biggest sporting event is the **Monaco Grand Prix** in May (*see page 66*); motor fans also come out for the **Monte**

Yachts galore

Vintage yawls, ketches, dragons and other classic racing yachts provide a spectacular vision as they set out across the Baie de Cannes at the end of September in **Les Régates Royales**, a regatta founded by the International Yacht Club of Cannes in 1929.

Carlo Car Rally in January, which finishes here after crossing the snow-covered Col de Turini. Nice and Monaco both have premier division **football** teams; horse racing takes place at the **Hippodrome de la Côte d'Azur** at Cagnes-sur-Mer just west of Nice. Other events include the **Monte Carlo Tennis Masters** men's singles tournament, international athletics meetings in Nice and Monaco, and international showjumping in Cannes and Monaco. The 1,200km (745-mile) **Paris–Nice cycling race** in mid-March, which finishes on the promenade des Anglais, is one of the big events of the international cycling calendar.

CHILDREN

Nice beach is a draw for children, although it is pebbly and shelves steeply; some private beaches have children's pools and sandpits. Treats include ice creams from **Fennocchio** on place Rossetti. **Parc Floral Phoenix** *(see page 43)* has plenty to keep kids amused, with an otter pool, aquariums with fish and spiders and a musical fountain. Local families also like the **Castel des Deux Rois**, east of the Vieux Port, which has good playgrounds, mini golf and water jets.

The main attractions at Cannes are the beach and the summer fireworks displays. The tourist-office brochure *Spécial Enfants* details activities (mainly in French) and child-friendly hotels (some have children's entertainments in July and August). **Ile Sainte-Marguerite** *(see page 59)* makes an ideal family day out, with beaches, picnic spots and an enjoyable boat trip at either end. There are also trips to be taken around the bay in glass-bottomed boats.

The aquarium in Monaco's **Musée Océanographique** *(see page 71)* is popular with families but gets crowded in July and August. The **doll museum** *(see page 66)* has an audience composed almost entirely of small girls; kids may also enjoy the cars in the **Collection de Voitures Anciennes** *(see page 74)*.

There's a **zoo** at Cap Ferrat (daily 9.30am–7pm; charge; www.zoocapferrat.com), between Nice and Monaco, with a lion reserve, panther canyon and breeding programmes for the endangered Madagascan lemur. The area's biggest attraction is **Marineland** (daily 10am–7pm, July–Aug until 11.30pm; charge; www.marineland.fr) between Antibes and Biot. Highlights are the whale and dolphin shows, but the complex also includes Aquasplash water park, Adventure Golf and La Petite Ferme du Far West, with baby farm animals and pony rides.

Having a whale of a time at Monaco's Musée Océanographique

Calendar of Events

January Monaco: Monte Carlo Car Rally cars hurtle from the Alps to the principality; Monaco Circus Festival; *Fête de Sainte-Dévote*.

February Nice: *Carnaval de Nice* (two weeks preceding Shrove Tuesday) *(see box page 86)*.

March Nice: Paris–Nice cycle race; *Festin des Cougourdins* in Cimiez, religious procession accompanied by strange gourds.

April Monaco: *Printemps des Arts* classical music and theatre festival; Monte Carlo Tennis Masters men's singles championship.

May Cannes: International Film Festival. Monaco: Monaco Grand Prix.

June France-wide (21st): *Fête de la Musique* free concerts, mostly outdoors. Nice: *Festival du Livre* literary festival; *Festival de la Musique Sacrée*. Monaco: international showjumping.

July France-wide (14th): Bastille Day, with dancing and fireworks. Nice: Nice Jazz Festival – first-rate performers in the Roman amphitheatre at Cimiez; festival lasts a week, usually in the second half of the month.

July–August Nice: *La Castellada* promenade spectacle on the castle hill. Cannes: Pantiero electronic music festival; *Les Nuits du Suquet* chamber music in front of the church; *Festival d'art pyrotechnique* spectacular fireworks. Monaco: Monte Carlo Sporting Festival – big-name pop, rock and soul stars perform at the Sporting d'Eté; *Cinéma d'Eté* outdoor cinema on a giant screen.

August Monaco: fireworks festival.

September France-wide (3rd weekend): *Journées du Patrimoine* heritage days. Cannes: International Yachting Festival luxury yacht salon, followed by *Les Régates Royales* classic yacht racing.

October Monaco: *Prix International d'Art Contemporain* winner's exhibition.

November Nice and Monaco: MANCA contemporary music festival. Monaco (18th, 19th): *Fête Nationale*. Nice and Cannes: *Marathon des Alpes-Maritimes* a scenic run between the promenade des Anglais in Nice and the Palais des Festivals in Cannes.

December Nice: *Lou Presèpi-Calena* live Christmas crib on place Rossetti. Cannes: dance festival (odd years).

EATING OUT

The south of France's exceptional local produce is at the heart of the cuisine here. Much of the best cooking is seasonal: asparagus in spring, all shapes and colours of tomatoes and courgettes in summer, tarts and gratins made with fresh figs in late summer, pumpkin soup, chestnuts, game, wild mushrooms and luxurious black truffles in autumn.

Regional Specialities

Olive oil rather than butter is used for cooking and is a crucial ingredient in *anchoïade* (also known as *bagna cauda*), a warm anchovy and olive oil sauce, into which chopped raw vegetables are dipped, and *aïoli* (garlic mayonnaise), which usually appears as an appetiser dip.

Salade niçoise

Nice's distinctive cuisine is a fusion of Provençal and Italianate influences resulting from the town's Savoyard past and a long to-and-fro history between the two, as well as its market-gardening tradition. Some specialities, such as *salade niçoise* (salad with tuna, olives, peppers, green beans, eggs and anchovies) and *ratatouille* (a luscious mixture of tomatoes, onions, garlic, courgettes, peppers and aubergines), have travelled the world; others remain essentially local.

Nice claims to have invented ravioli, but here, unlike those found in Italy, they are typically filled with leftover *daube de bœuf* (beef stewed in red wine and herbs) and swiss chard. Other Italianate specialities include gnocchi, made from potatoes or durum wheat, and *soupe au pistou*, a minestrone-like vegetable and bean soup into which a dollop of basil pesto is stirred at the end. Nice's *cailletier* olive turns up in many dishes; indeed, *à la niçoise* on a menu will often indicate a sauce made with tomatoes, onions and black olives, and may be found accompanying pasta, fish, chicken or rabbit. Perhaps the most characteristic of all Niçois dishes, however, is *petits farcis niçois*, an assortment of stuffed tomatoes, aubergines, courgettes, onions and bell peppers, each with its own slightly different filling, based around ham, rice, herbs, minced meat and breadcrumbs.

Portable Treats

Snack food is an art form in Nice, where a whole range of specialities just seem designed for eating in the street. *Socca*, one of the legendary dishes sold at stalls in Vieux Nice (best-known are Chez René Socca and Chez Thérèse at the market), is a thin chickpea crêpe cooked on a large circular iron plaque, then cut up into portions, seasoned with black pepper, and best served very hot; *pissaladière* is a delicious open onion tart, garnished with anchovy fillets and black olives. Then there are *panisses*, deep-fried chickpea flour fritters, and *ganses*, mini doughnuts flavoured with orange blossom water and dusted with icing sugar, traditionally eaten during the Carnaval period. Even *salade niçoise* has its portable version, the *pan bagnat*: a crusty roll rubbed with garlic and olive oil and crammed with lettuce, tomato, onion, tuna and anchovies.

Vegetable Heaven

One area where Niçois and Provençal cuisine differ from the rest of France is the emphasis on vegetables, thanks both to the variety and quality of local produce and to peasant tradition where meat was mainly reserved for special occasions. Preparations can be as gloriously simple as marinated and roasted red peppers, or the fresh herbs and varied young

Peppers and garlic are two local staples

salad leaves of delicate *mesclun*. Tomatoes are an ingredient in numerous sauces, but also appear as simple salads and chilled summer soups or as *tomates provençales*, a popular accompaniment to meat and fish dishes, sprinkled with minced garlic and breadcrumbs and baked very slowly until almost caramelised. Look out also for *caponata*, aubergine stewed with tomatoes and capers.

You'll also find all manner of vegetable *tians*, baked gratins of courgette, squash or aubergine with egg and rice, named after the rectangular earthenware dish in which they are cooked. Tiny purple artichokes, almost without a choke, are braised *à la barigoule* with mushrooms and bacon, but are also sliced very finely and eaten raw. Another treat is delicate orangey-yellow courgette flowers, dipped in egg and flour and deep-fried as fritters or stuffed with *brousse* (fresh cheese). *Blettes* (swiss chard) are served as a vegetable or combined with apples, raisins and pine kernels in Nice's *tourte de blettes*, a surprisingly sweet tart; while stuffed cabbage, the leaves bound around a sausage-meat filling, is a rustic speciality of the Cannes and Grasse area.

Fresh seafood is a regional speciality

Fish and Meat

Not surprisingly, given the Côte d'Azur's glorious coastline and the trend for healthy eating, fish plays a large role, especially at beach restaurants and around the Vieux Port in Nice; though overfishing of the Mediterranean and the decline of the Riviera's fishing fleet mean that apart from the grandest restaurants, which still buy directly from the remaining local fishermen, much of the fish now comes from France's Breton and Atlantic ports.

Sardines are a speciality in Nice, stuffed with Swiss chard, marinated or grilled, as is *estocaficada* (*stockfisch* in Cannes, *stocafi* in Monaco), salt cod stewed in wine with tomatoes and olives. You'll find the fish stew *bouillabaisse* (originally from Marseille) all along the coast, served in two courses, first the saffron-coloured soup accompanied by a garlicky *rouille* and then the fish and potatoes. Other typical preparations include sea bream baked with fennel and red mullet with basil, as well as grander dishes like sea bass baked in a crust of sea salt. For a brief period in spring look out for the local delicacy *poutine*, the tiny fry of sardines and anchovies fished with nets on the beach (now authorised only between 15 February and 31 March), which is prepared in soup, omelettes or fritters.

Meat is not forgotten, however – this is France. Almost every brasserie will have a *steak frites* on its menu, or a succulent Provençal *daube de bœuf*, stewed in red wine and herbs with a touch of orange zest. Rabbit is also commonly found, roasted with herbs or cooked *à la niçoise* with white wine, olives and tomatoes. The best lamb comes comes from the Alpine hinterland, notably Sisteron, while a more challenging Provençal classic is *pieds et paquets*, stuffed sheep's tripe and feet stewed for hours in a tomato sauce.

Cheese and Desserts

The Côte d'Azur is not a major cheese-making area, but you will find some mountain-style cow's-milk cheeses from the Mercantour as well as goat's cheese *(chèvre)*, ranging from young, moist, fresh cheeses to harder, drier *crottins*. Among specialities are *poivre d'âne*, goat's cheese rolled in summer savory, tiny cheeses marinated in olive oil and herbs, and *brousse*, a ricotta-like fresh cheese used in dips and desserts.

Desserts are mostly based around fruit, including figs baked in tarts, gratins and crumbles, and lemon me-

Crêpe Suzette

According to legend, the crêpe Suzette was created in 1896 at Monte Carlo's Café de Paris, especially for the Prince of Wales who was dining there with a companion named Suzette. In one version, they were invented accidentally by Escoffier when a crêpe doused in orange liqueur caught fire; in another, by a 14-year-old waiter, Henri Charpentier.

ringue tart *(tarte au citron meringué)* made with little lemons from nearby Menton. Fashionable desserts include summer-fruit soups and creations inspired by nostalgia for children's caramel bars and strawberry sweets.

Where to Eat

Restaurants in France range from informal bistros with a convivial atmosphere, tightly packed tables and regional specialities, via modern gourmet bistros and fashionable designer venues, to grand haute-cuisine establishments, with superb cuisine, starched linen and formal service.

Brasseries typically keep long hours – some serve all day – and have a lively atmosphere and a menu of classics, such as grilled fish and meat or gleaming platters of oysters and shellfish. There are also numerous Italian restaurants, ranging from popular pizzerias to authentic trattorias. At lunch,

Evening dining in Nice

the French will often eat casually in a café, perhaps the *plat du jour* (hot dish of the day) or a salad, and even in smarter restaurants may opt for just a starter and main course or main course and dessert rather than all three.

Many restaurants in Vieux Nice and Le Suquet in Cannes remain firmly attached to tradition, with checked tablecloths and menus of regional specialities that don't seem to have changed for decades, but, happily, southern cuisine continues to evolve. In Nice's New Town, a growing number of chefs, often with an haute-cuisine background, are making adventurous use of regional produce and bringing in cosmopolitan infuences (Keisuke Matsushima, for instance, is Japanese and trained with Régis Marcon and the Pourcel twins, while Luc Salsedo worked at Alain Ducasse's Louis XV and the Chèvre d'Or in Eze but has chosen to go for a market menu that changes every 10 days). At such places, you might find modern experimental preparations – magenta-coloured beetroot purées, lots of raw carpaccios and layered *millefeuilles* alongside a return to roots, with slow cooking in cast-iron casseroles.

Grand haute-cuisine estabishments, such as Le Chantecler in Nice and Louis XV in Monte Carlo, remain a pinnacle for special-occasion dining with luxurious ingredients and splendid settings, but Alain Llorca, who has taken over the Moulin de Mougins, where his predecessor Roger Vivier was a pioneer of nouvelle cuisine, has brought in a 'tapas menu' alongside the more classic *carte*, while Jouni Tormanen at the elegant Réserve de Nice has followed the Parisian trend for bistro annexes by opening a casual cosmpolitan bistro in the same premises.

A notable trend in Nice is for wine bars and wine bistros, where one feature is well-chosen wines available by the glass. Old-style wine bars concentrated largely on simple plates of charcuterie and cheeses, but the new breed often produce adventurous modern dishes but served in a less formal atmosphere than in conventional restaurants.

What to Drink

Something you'll probably only ever see on a wine list in Nice are the rare Bellet wines, produced on the outskirts of the city. Most wine lists will also have a good choice from the rest of Provence, including Côtes de Provence, in all three colours; vast quantities of light, summery rosé; more substantial Bandol wines and the southern Rhône appellations – Côtes du Luberon, Châteauneuf-du-Pape and Coteaux d'Aix-en-Provence. As well as 75cl bottles, wine bars will often have a good choice by the glass, while bistros may offer wines in 25cl or 50cl carafes.

Local grapes produce light wines

To Help You Order...

Do you have a table?	**Avez-vous une table?**
I'd like some...	**Je voudrais du/de la/des...**
The bill, please	**L'addition, s'il vous plaît**

bread	**pain**	pepper	**poivre**
butter	**beurre**	salt	**sel**
cheese	**fromage**	sugar	**sucre**
coffee	**café**	tea	**thé**
fish	**poisson**	water	**de l'eau**
fruit	**fruit**	mineral water	**eau minérale**
ice cream	**glace**	still	**plate**
meat	**viande**	fizzy	**gazeuse**
milk	**lait**	wine	**vin**

...and Read the Menu

agneau	lamb	**jambon**	ham
ail	garlic	**lapin**	rabbit
ananas	pineapple	**légumes**	vegetables
anchois	anchovy	**lotte**	monkfish
asperges	asparagus	**loup**	sea bass
bar	sea bass	**morue**	salt cod
beignet	fritter	**œufs**	eggs
blette	swiss chard	**pâte**	pastry
bœuf	beef	**pâtes**	pasta
cabillaud	cod	**pêche**	peach
caille	quail	**pintade**	guinea fowl
canard	duck	**poire**	pear
câpre	caper	**poireau**	leek
cerise	cherry	**pomme**	apple
champignon	mushroom	**pomme**	
chou	cabbage	**de terre**	potato
crevette	prawn/shrimp	**poulet**	chicken
daube	stew	**poulpe**	octopus
daurade	sea bream	**prune**	plum
dinde	turkey	**pruneau**	prune
épinards	spinach	**raisin**	grape
espadon	swordfish	**rascasse**	scorpion fish
farci	stuffed	**rognons**	kidneys
fève	broad bean	**rouget**	red mullet
foie	liver	**saint-pierre**	john dory
fraises	strawberries	**saucisse**	sausage
framboises	raspberries	**saumon**	salmon
friture	whitebait	**thon**	tuna
fruits de mer	shellfish	**truite**	trout
gibier	game	**veau**	veal
homard	lobster	**velouté**	creamy soup
huîtres	oysters	**volaille**	poultry

HANDY TRAVEL TIPS

An A–Z Summary of Practical Information

A Accommodation . . 107
Airports 108
B Bicycle Hire 110
Budgeting for
Your Trip 110
C Car Hire 111
Climate 111
Clothing 112
Crime and Safety . . 112
Customs and Entry
Requirements . . . 112
D Driving 113
E Electricity 114
Embassies and
Consulates 115
Emergencies 115
G Gay and Lesbian
Travellers 115
Getting There 115
Guides and Tours . . 116
H Health and
Medical Care . . . 117

Holidays 118
L Language 119
Laundry and
Dry-Cleaning . . . 119
M Maps 119
Media 120
Money 120
O Opening Hours . . . 121
P Police 122
Post Offices 122
Public Transport . . 123
R Religion 123
S Smoking 124
T Telephones 124
Time Zones 125
Tipping 125
Toilets 125
Tourist
Information 125
W Websites and
Internet 126
Y Youth Hostels 126

A

ACCOMMODATION (See also YOUTH HOSTELS, and the list of Recommended Hotels on page 127)

Hotels. Nice and Cannes have an impressive range of accommodation to suit all budgets. Monaco has a more limited number of mainly large luxury hotels. All three cities become very booked up in July and August and during major events. In late May, during Cannes Film Festival and the Monaco Grand Prix, hotels for miles around hike up their prices and are often booked months ahead.

France has an official rating system from one to four stars and four-star luxe, based on criteria such as size of room and presence of a lift, and not on qualities such as cleanliness, tasteful decoration or warmth of welcome, nor on more recent facilities, such as internet access. Even most two-star hotels now have en suite bathrooms and air conditioning. Luxury hotels will have 24-hour room service and offer all sorts of services, from DVD players and business centres to yacht and helicopter hire. An updated rating system is due to be introduced.

If booking ahead, the hotel may ask for a deposit, or *arrhes*, but is more likely to request your credit card number. Reservations will usually be honoured until 6pm, but may be given to another client if you have not arrived, or telephoned to explain, before that time.

If looking for last-minute accommodation, the tourist offices in Nice, Cannes and Monaco have a direct booking service.

Most hotels in Nice and Cannes are independently owned, though some are affiliated to groups, such as Best Western (www.best western.com), Châteaux & Hôtels Collection (www.chateauxhotels. com), Exclusive Hotels (www.exclusive-hotels.com) and Leading Hotels of the World (www.lhw.com). There are also hotels belonging to the Accor group (Sofitel, Mercure, Novotel, Suite Hotel, Ibis, Etap; www.accorhotels.com) and Louvre Hotels (Kyriad, Campanile, Première Classe chains; www.louvrehotels.com). The majority of Monaco hotels belong to the Société des Bains de Monaco (www.montecarloresort.com) or to international groups.

Chambres d'hôtes are bed and breakfast rooms in a private home; originally a rural phenomenon, but there are also some *chambres d'hôtes* in towns – enquire at the tourist office.

Appart'hôtels/Résidences de tourisme/Résidences hôtelières. Complexes of holiday studios and apartments, with kitchens.

Villas and seaside flats. Numerous agencies rent villas and holiday flats, ranging from luxury villas with maid service to simple studios.

Youth hostels. *See page 126.*

Do you have a single/ double room for tonight?	**Avez-vous une chambre simple/double pour ce soir?**
with double/twin beds	**avec grand lit/avec deux lits**
with bath/shower/toilet	**avec bain/douche/toilette**
What is the rate per night?	**Quel est le prix pour une nuit?**

AIRPORTS *(aéroports)*

Aéroport Nice-Côte d'Azur, on the western edge of Nice, is France's second-busiest airport (tel: 08 20 42 33 33/04 93 21 30 30, www. nice.aeroport.fr). There are connections to all major European cities, North Africa and some American cities. There are numerous flights from the UK with both national and low-cost airlines:

Air France (UK tel: 0870 142 4343, France tel: 08 20 82 08 20, www.airfrance.com) flights from London Heathrow and Paris.

Bmi (UK tel: 0870 607 0555, France tel: 01 55 69 83 06, www.fly bmi.com) flights from Birmingham.

Bmibaby (UK tel: 0871 224 0224, France tel: 08 90 71 00 81, www.bmibaby.com) flights from Birmingham, East Midlands and Heathrow.

British Airways (UK tel: 0844 493 0787, France tel: 08 25 82 54 00, www.britishairways.com) flights from Heathrow, Manchester and Birmingham.

easyJet (UK tel: 0905 821 0905, France tel: 08 99 65 00 11, www. easyjet.com) flights from Belfast, Bristol, Edinburgh, Gatwick, Liverpool, Luton, Newcastle and Stansted.

Flybe (UK tel: 01392 268 529, www.flybe.com) flights from Exeter, Jersey and Southampton.

Flyglobespan (UK tel: 08705 561522, www.flyglobespan.com) flights from Edinburgh.

Jet2 (tel: 0871 226 1737, www.jet2.com) flights from Leeds and Manchester.

Ryanair (Ireland tel: 0818 303030/01 249 7791, France tel: 08 92 23 23 75, www.ryanair.com) flights from Dublin.

Transport from the airport

RCA buses depart from Nice airport for all main destinations along the coast. Buy tickets before boarding at the car park/bus cash desk inside the terminals. There is a free shuttle between the terminals and the car parks.

- Line 23 from Terminal 1 to northern Nice via Gambetta and Nice railway station, Mon–Sat 6.10am–9.35pm, Sun from 7.05am.
- Line 98 from Terminals 1 and 2 direct to Nice bus station (gare routière), daily 5.59am–11.37pm.
- Line 99 from Terminals 1 and 2 direct to Nice railway station (Gare SNCF), daily 7.53am–8.53pm.
- Line 110 Aéroport–Monte Carlo–Menton Express along the motorway from Terminals 1 and 2, daily 9am–9.15pm.
- Line 200 to Cannes by RN7 from Terminal 1, Mon–Sat 7.20am–10pm, Sun 8.05am–9.55pm, every 30–40 mins, less in the evening.

Taxi with Central Taxi Riviera from Terminals 1 and 2, tel: 04 93 13 78 78; typical fares central Nice €25–30, Cannes €70–75, Monaco €75–85.

Motorbike taxi with Easy Moov (tel: 04 93 00 12 60, www.easymoov.fr), set fares: Nice airport to Nice €28, to Cannes €58, to Monaco €65.

Heli Air Monaco (tel: +377-92 05 00 50, www.heliairmonaco.com) scheduled helicopter services between Nice airport and Monaco take 6 minutes, and are not necessarily much more expensive than a taxi. Nice–Monaco €115; Monaco-Nice €99.

B

BICYCLE HIRE

Elite Rent a Bike 32 avenue Maréchal Juin, Cannes, tel: 04 93 94 30 34, www.elite-rentabike.com. Bicycles, scooters and motorbikes.
Holiday Bikes 34 avenue Auber, Nice, tel: 04 93 16 01 62 and 21–23 rue du Canada, Cannes, tel: 04 97 06 07 07, www.holiday-bikes.com. Bicycles, electricity-assisted bikes, scooters and motorbikes.
Roller Station 49 quai des Etats-Unis, Nice, tel: 04 93 62 99 05, www.roller-station.com. Bicycles and in-line skates.

BUDGETING FOR YOUR TRIP

The following are approximate prices in euros (€):
Bicycle hire. €12–20 per day, deposit €100–450.
Car hire. €25–50 a day for an economy model, from €180 per week. There are often good deals if you book at the same time as a flight or train.
Entertainment. Cinema €8–9. Nightclub/casino admission often 'free' but a premium on drinks. Opera ticket €8–80.
Meals and drinks. Breakfast €6–30 depending on category of hotel. In restaurants in the evening expect to pay around €20 for three courses, not including wine, in a budget establishment, €25–35 in a good bistro, €30–60 in a trendy beachside establishment, €80 or more in a top gastronomic restaurant. Coffee €1.50–2.50; 25cl beer €2.50–3; sandwich in a café €3.50; salad in a café €8–12.
Museums. Nice's municipal museums are free; other museums €3–8.
Private beach. Day on a sun lounger with parasol €15–40.

C

CAR HIRE (*location de voitures;* see also DRIVING)

The major car-hire companies all have branches at Nice airport; most also have branches in Nice (around the train station), Cannes and Monaco. To hire a car, you must have a driving licence (held for at least one year) and a passport. The minimum age varies from 20 to 23. A substantial deposit (refundable) may be required, but most companies swipe your credit card. You will be asked for proof of your local address. Third-party insurance is compulsory. Major car-hire companies include:

Avis: tel: 08 20 05 05 05, www.avis.com

Budget: tel: 08 25 00 35 64, www.budget.com

Europcar: tel: 08 25 358 358, www.europcar.com

Hertz: tel: 01 39 38 38 38, www.hertz-europe.com

Rent-a-Car: tel: 08 91 70 02 00, www.rentacar.fr

Several companies also offer luxury car hire:

Calandres (Monaco): tel: +377-93 50 25 25, www.calandres.mc

Elite Rent-a-Car: tel: (France) 04 93 94 61 00, (Monaco) +377-97 77 33 11, www.eliterent.com. Sports cars and luxury limos with or without chauffeur.

I'd like to rent a car today/tomorrow for one day/ the weekend/a week	**Je voudrais louer une voiture aujourd'hui/demain pour une journée/ le week-end/une semaine**

CLIMATE

The French Riviera enjoys a typical Mediterranean climate, with hot, dry summers, mild and wet weather in spring and autumn, and short winters that are usually mild, with occasional cold spells. There are often thunderstorms at night in late August or in September. Here are some average monthly temperatures, but note that peak daytime temperatures can be over 35°C (95°F) in July and August:

		J	F	M	A	M	J	J	A	S	O	N	D
Air	°C	9	9	11	13	17	20	23	22	20	17	12	9
	°F	48	48	52	55	63	68	73	72	68	63	54	48
Sea	°C	13	13	13	15	17	21	24	25	23	20	17	14
	°F	55	55	55	59	63	70	75	77	73	68	63	57

CLOTHING

Cannes and Monaco are the most dressed-up places on the Côte d'Azur, but only the grandest restaurants and casinos require men to wear a jacket and tie *(tenue correcte)*. Elsewhere smart casual attire is the norm. Avoid shorts for dining out at night and trainers if you want to get into exclusive nightclubs. In Monaco you are not allowed to walk around the streets in swimwear, and respectable attire is required for religious buildings. Even in summer, a sweater or wrap is useful for cooler evenings, and a waterproof coat or jacket will be needed from October to April.

CRIME AND SAFETY (See also EMERGENCIES and POLICE)

Inevitably, such a prosperous area attracts petty criminals, and the three cities have some security problems, but incidents of violent crime against visitors are rare. Try not to carry large amounts of cash, never leave valuables in your car, and be on the lookout for pickpockets, especially in crowds. Any loss or theft should be reported immediately to the nearest *commissariat de police*.

CUSTOMS (la douane) AND ENTRY REQUIREMENTS

British visitors need only a passport to enter France, as do nationals of other EU countries and Switzerland. US citizens do not need a visa for stays of up to 90 days. Others should check with the French Embassy in their country for entry requirements.

As France is part of the EU, free exchange of non-duty-free goods for personal use is permitted between France and the UK and the Republic of Ireland. However, duty-free items are still subject to restrictions – check before you go.

For residents of non-EU countries, the restrictions into France and back into your own country are as follows: **France:** 200 cigarettes or 50 cigars or 250g tobacco, 1l spirits and 2l wine; **Australia:** 250 cigarettes or 250g of tobacco, 1l alcohol; **Canada:** 200 cigarettes and 50 cigars and 400g of tobacco, 1.1l spirits or wine or 8.5l beer; **New Zealand:** 200 cigarettes or 50 cigars or 250g tobacco, 4.5l wine or beer and 1.1l spirits; **South Africa:** 200 cigarettes and 50 cigars and 250g tobacco, 2l wine and 1l spirits; **US:** 200 cigarettes or 50 cigars or 2kg tobacco, 1l wine or spirits.

D

DRIVING (See also CAR HIRE)

To take a car into France you'll need a valid driving licence, your car registration papers, insurance coverage and a set of spare bulbs. A red warning triangle and a fluorescent safety waistcoat are obligatory in case of breakdown. Drivers and all passengers (back and front) are required by law to wear seatbelts (where fitted in the back). Children under 10 may not travel in the front of the car other than in appropriate baby seats with the air bag disconnected. Driving with a foreign provisional licence is not permitted. The minimum driving age is 18.

Driving regulations. Drive on the right, pass on the left. In built-up areas, give priority to vehicles coming from the right unless indicated by road markings. At a roundabout, drivers already on the roundabout have priority over those entering it, unless it is marked *priorité à droite*.

Speed limits. When conditions are dry, the limit is 130km/h (80mph) on *autoroutes* (motorways/expressways), 110km/h (70mph) on dual carriageways (divided highways), 90km/h (55mph) on other country roads, 50km/h (30mph) in built-up areas and 30km/h (20mph) in some residential districts. Speed limits are reduced in wet weather. There are speed radars installed on some roads.

Routes and road conditions. The A8 motorway runs west–east across the Côte d'Azur; you can also take the N7 and N98 between Nice and Cannes and the three scenic but twisty Corniches between Nice and Monaco: the Basse (low) Corniche or Corniche Inférieure (N98), Moyenne (middle) Corniche (N7) and the Grande Corniche (D2564). Roads can get very clogged up in summer, especially on Saturdays and around the 14 July and 15 August public holidays.

Parking *(stationnement)*. It's wisest to park in an underground car park. If your hotel does not have its own car park, it may have preferential tariffs at a public one. On-street parking is usually on pay-and-display ticket machines. *Stationnement interdit* means 'no parking'. *Sauf riverains* means 'except residents'. Don't leave a car in a *zone piétonne* (pedestrian zone), or where a sign says *stationnement gênant* (parking obstructive), or it may be towed away.

Fuel and oil *(essence; huile)*. Unleaded petrol is *essence sans plomb* and diesel is *gasoil*. Most fuel stations are self-service. It's worth filling up on Saturday, since many garages close on Sunday, although large supermarkets often have 24-hour petrol pumps for use with credit cards. Fuel tends to be more expensive on motorways.

ELECTRICITY

220-volt, 50-cycle AC is universal. British visitors should remember to buy an adaptor *(adaptateur)*; American visitors will need a transformer *(transformateur)*.

EMBASSIES AND CONSULATES

Most are open from Monday to Friday, from 9 or 10am to 4 or 5pm with an hour or so off for lunch. Most are in Paris or Marseille.

Australia: (Embassy) 4 rue Jean-Rey, 75015 Paris, tel: 01 40 50 33 00, www.france.embassy.gov.au

Canada: (Consulate) 35 avenue Montaigne, 75008 Paris, tel: 01 44 43 29 02, www.international.gc.ca

Ireland: (Embassy) 12 avenue Foch, 75116 Paris, tel: 01 44 17 67 00, www.embassyofirelandparis.com

UK: (Consulate) 24 avenue du Prado, Marseille 13006, tel: 04 91 15 72 10, http://ukinfrance.fco.gov.uk

US: (Consulate) 7 avenue Gustave V, 06000 Nice, tel: 04 93 88 89 55, http://france.usembassy.gov/consulara.html

EMERGENCIES *(urgences;* see also HEALTH and POLICE)

In case of an emergency, dial **15** for an ambulance (SAMU), dial **17** for the police *(police-secours)* and **18** for the fire brigade *(sapeurs-pompiers)*. Dial **112** from a mobile phone.

G

GAY AND LESBIAN TRAVELLERS

Nice and Cannes are gay-tolerant cities with several gay bars and clubs; Coco Beach east of Nice's Vieux Port is a popular gay beach. *Nice Practical Guide* and *www Cannes*, published by the respective tourist offices, list gay and gay-friendly bars and hotels. There's a lively Gay Pride parade in June in Nice.

GETTING THERE (See also AIRPORTS)

By car. The 1,200km (750-mile) *autoroute* trip from Calais to Nice (via Reims and bypassing Paris) can take as little as 15 hours. However, *péage* (toll) fees are expensive. For toll estimates and route-planning, see www.mappy.fr or www.viamichelin.fr.

By bus. The cheapest way to get to the Riviera is by bus. Eurolines (UK tel: 01582 404511, France tel: 08 92 69 52 52, www.eurolines. com) has services from London to Cannes and Nice.

By train. From the UK, Eurostar trains (tel: 08705 186186, www. eurostar.co.uk) run from London St Pancras, Ebbsfleet and Ashford International to Lille and Paris Gare du Nord (to Paris only from Ashford). Services for the South depart from the Gare de Lyon. The high-speed TGV reaches Nice in six hours; some trains also stop at Cannes and Monaco. It is also possible to change trains at Lille. In the UK, tickets can be booked at the Rail Europe Travel Centre (1 Regent Street, London SW1 4XT, tel: 08448 484 064/051) or online at www. raileurope.co.uk. For SNCF reservations and information, France tel: 3635, www.voyages-sncf.com. US visitors can call 877 257 2887 or visit www.raileurope.com/us. Enquire about passes and discounts.

By motor-rail. Between May and September, the SNCF operates a direct service from Calais to Nice (tel: 08448 484 050, www.rail europe.co.uk), and all year round if you travel separately from your car from Paris and Lille.

GUIDES AND TOURS *(guides; excursions)*

Walking tours. A two-hour guided tour of Vieux Nice in French and English leaves from the main tourist office every Saturday at 9.30am (reserve). The Centre du Patrimoine (75 quai des Etats-Unis, Nice, tel: 04 92 00 41 90, www.nice.fr) organises regular Heritage walking tours of Nice; in English by appointment.

Nice Le Grand Tour. A 90-minute tour of the city on a double-decker bus with the possibility of getting on and off at any of the 11 stops.

Boat trips *(see also Iles de Lérins, page 58).* Aquavision (tel: +377-92 16 15 15, www.aquavision-monaco.com) – hour-long trips along the coat from Monaco's Port Hercule. Horizon (tel: 04 92 98 71, www.cannes-horizon.com) – hour-long trips from Cannes in a glass-bottomed catamaran.

Trans Côte d'Azur (tel: 04 92 00 42 30) – trips from Nice to Villefranche-sur-Mer.

Helicopter tours. Héli Air Monaco (tel: +377-92 05 00 50, www.heli airmonaco.com) – 10-minute panoramic tours of the principality.

Tourist mini trains. Sightseeing circuits with commentary in several languages: Petit Train Nice (www.petittrainnice.com) from the promenade des Anglais (Jardin Albert I) through Vieux Nice and up Castle Hill; Cannes Cinema Tour (tel: 04 93 38 39 18, www. cannes-petit-train.com) from the Palais des Festivals around Le Suquet or along La Croisette; Azur Express (tel: +377-92 05 64 38) leaving from the Musée Océanographique.

Day trips. Several companies offer half-day and whole-day tours to sights such as Saint-Paul-de-Vence or Gourdon, or further afield to the spectacular Gorges du Verdon or Aix-en-Provence, including Tour Azur (coach or minibus trips from Nice and Cannes; tel: 04 93 44 88 77, www.tourazur.com) and Med Tour (minibus tours from Nice; tel: 04 93 82 92 58, www.med-tour.com).

H

HEALTH AND MEDICAL CARE (See also EMERGENCIES)

EU nationals are entitled to use the French Social Security system, which refunds up to 70 percent of medical expenses. To get a refund, British nationals should obtain a European Health Insurance Card before leaving the UK. These are available online at www. ehic.org.uk or from post offices. If you have treatment while in France, the doctor will give you a prescription and a *feuille de soins* (statement of treatment). The medication will carry *vignettes* (stickers), which you attach to your *feuille de soins*. Send this, the prescription and details of your EHI Card to the local Caisse Primaire d'Assurance Maladie (in the phone book under Sécurité Sociale). Refunds can take over a month. Nationals of non-EU countries should have private medical insurance.

Your hotel can probably recommend an English-speaking doctor or dentist. Chemists *(pharmacies)* display green crosses. Staff are helpful in dealing with minor ailments and can recommend a nurse *(infirmière)* if you need other care. The address of duty chemists open on Sunday and at night is displayed in pharmacies – the police station or local papers will also have it. There is an all-night pharmacy in Nice at 7 rue Masséna.

24-hour casualty departments *(Urgences)*:

Nice: Centre Hospitalier Universitaire (CHU) Saint-Roch, 5 rue Pierre Dévoluy, Nice, tel: 04 92 03 33 33.

Monaco: Centre Hospitalier Princesse Grace, 1 avenue Pasteur, Monaco, tel: +377-97 98 97 69.

Where is the nearest pharmacy?	**Où est la pharmacie la plus proche?**
Please call a doctor/dentist	**Appelez un médecin/ un dentiste, s'il vous plaît**

HOLIDAYS *(jours fériés)*

In France, banks, public buildings, and most museums and shops close on public holidays, and transport often runs on Sunday schedules; some holidays are more widely observed than others, notably 1 January, 1 May, 14 July and 25 December.

1 January	**Jour de l'An**	New Year's Day
March/April	**Lundi de Pâques**	Easter Monday
1 May	**Fête du Travail**	Labour Day
8 May	**Fête de la Libération**	Victory Day (1945)
May	**Jeudi de l'Ascension**	Ascension Thursday
May/June	**Lundi de Pentecôte**	Whit Monday
14 July	**Fête Nationale**	Bastille Day
15 August	**Assomption**	Assumption
1 November	**Toussaint**	All Saints' Day

| 11 November | **Anniversaire de l'Armistice** | Armistice Day |
| 25 December | **Noël** | Christmas |

In Monaco many museums close for the Monaco Grand Prix in May. Additional holidays in Monaco are:

27 January	**Fête de Sainte Dévote**	St Devota's Day
May	**Fête-Dieu**	Corpus Christi
19 November	**Fête Nationale**	Monaco National Holiday

L

LANGUAGE

Southern French has a warm, pleasing accent, drawing out syllables and placing extra emphasis on the ends of words or sentences. The usual nasal French 'en' ending becomes a hard 'ng' (*chien* sounds like *chieng*). In addition, in Vieux Nice you may see bilingual street names and hear Nissart, an old Occitan Provençal dialect that is going through a bit of a fashionable revival. French is the official language in Monaco, but Italian and English are also widely spoken; you may also come across Monégasque (an Italian dialect).

LAUNDRY AND DRY-CLEANING

There are plenty of overnight dry-cleaners *(un pressing)*, and many hotels have laundry services. There are self-service launderettes *(laveries automatiques)* in Nice and Cannes but none in Monaco, where the nearest launderette is in Menton.

M

MAPS

The tourist offices in Nice, Cannes and Monaco can all provide a town street map *(un plan)*, as can most hotels.

MEDIA

Newspapers *(journaux)*. *Nice Matin* is the principal regional daily; the main French nationals (*Le Monde*, *Libération*, *Le Figaro*) are also widely available; there is also a Nice version of the free newspaper *Métro*.

British newspapers and magazines can be found at many newsstands, as can the Paris-based *International Herald Tribune* and *USA Today*. There's a particularly wide selection of international newspapers at the Maison de la Presse at 1 place Masséna in Nice. Look out for the English-language glossy magazine *Riviera Reporter* (www.riviera-reporter.com), which gives an irreverent, insider's view of the region, and the monthly *The Riviera Times*.

Television and radio. France has five main TV channels (TF1, France 2, France 3, Arte, M6), plus the subscription channel Canal+, and numerous cable and satellite channels, often including BBC World or CNN. National radio stations include France Inter (FM 100.2 MHz), France Info (FM 105.7 MHz) and France Musiques (FM 92.2 MHz); RFI (Radio France International) has English-language bulletins; Europe 1 (101.4 MHz) is a good news and general channel; Nostalgie (FM 93.5 MHz) and NRJ (FM 99.2 MHz) are popular music channels; BBC World Service is available at certain times of day on short-wave radio. Monte Carlo's Riviera Radio (106.3 MHz in Monaco and 106.5 in southern France) is an all-English station, broadcasting news, weather, finance and yachting info, as well as pop hits and oldies.

MONEY

Currency *(monnaie)*. The unit of currency in both France and Monaco is the euro (€), divided into 100 cents. Banknotes are available in denominations of 500, 200, 100, 50, 20, 10 and 5 euros (many shops will not accept €200 and €500 notes). There are coins for 2 and 1 euros and for 50, 20, 10, 5, 2 and 1 cent.

ATMs. ATMs are plentiful in large cities and are the easiest, and usually cheapest, way of obtaining cash in euros, drawn on either your debit or credit card.

Banks and currency-exchange offices (*banques; bureaux de change*). Not all banks have exchange facilities; look for those with a change sign. Most banks open Monday to Friday 9am–noon, 2–5pm; some open on Saturday morning and close on Monday. Big hotels will usually change currency, but the rate is often not favourable. Travellers' cheques are not widely used; it is easier to withdraw money from bank machines with a credit card.

Credit cards (*cartes de crédit*). Most hotels, restaurants, shops, car-hire firms, motorway toll booths and petrol stations accept major credit cards, especially Visa and MasterCard. There may be a minimum sum (often €15).

Lost and stolen credit cards: Groupement des Cartes Bancaires tel: 0892 70 57 05; American Express tel: 01 47 77 72 00; Diners Club tel: 0810 31 41 59; Eurocard/MasterCard tel: 0800 90 13 87; Visa tel: 08 92 70 57 05.

Could you give me some change?	**Pouvez-vous me donner de la monnaie?**
I want to change some pounds/dollars.	**Je voudrais changer des livres sterling/des dollars.**
Do you accept travellers' cheques/credit cards?	**Prenez-vous les chèques de voyage/cartes de crédit?**

OPENING HOURS (*heures d'ouverture*)

Shops generally open Mon–Sat 9.30 or 10am to 7pm; small shops often take a long lunch break, from noon to 3 or 4pm; bakeries generally open 8am–8pm and may open on Sunday, with one closing day a week; some supermarkets open until 9 or 10pm.

Banks usually open Mon–Fri 9am–noon, 2–5pm. Some close on Monday and open on Saturday morning. Banking facilities are available at Nice airport from early morning to late at night (depending on flight arrivals and departures).

Post. Nice's main post office, opposite the train station on avenue Thiers, is open Mon–Fri 8am–7pm and Sat 8am–noon; smaller post offices usually open Mon–Fri 9am–noon, 2–5pm, Sat 9am–noon.

Museums usually open 10am–6pm and often close on Monday or Tuesday; smaller ones may close at lunchtime.

P

POLICE *(la police)*

Theft should be reported to the Police Nationale in Nice and Cannes or to the Gendarmerie in smaller towns and rural areas. Monaco has its own, highly visible police force.

Call **17** anywhere in France for police assistance.

Commissariat Central Nice, 1 avenue Maréchal Foch, Nice, tel: 04 92 17 22 22.

Lost property *(objets trouvés)*: 1 rue de la Terrasse, Nice, tel: 04 97 13 44 10.

Commissariat de Police, 1 avenue de Grasse, Cannes, tel: 04 93 06 22 22.

Direction de la Sûreté Publique (Police), 3 rue Louis Notari, Monaco; tel: +377-93 15 30 15; lost property +377-93 15 30 18.

POST OFFICES

Post offices display a sign with a stylised bluebird and the words La Poste. In addition to normal mail service, you can buy *télécartes* (phone cards), and receive or send money. If just sending letters and small packages, it is quicker to use the automatic stamp machines than to queue for service. You can also buy stamps *(timbres)* and *télécartes* at tobacconists *(tabacs)*. Monaco has its own stamps.

PUBLIC TRANSPORT

By bus and tram. Nice has a comprehensive network of urban bus routes and a tramway run by Ligne d'Azur (www.lignedazur.com), plus four night-bus routes leaving from place Masséna. Single journeys have a flat rate of €1 (allowing one change), which can be bought on the bus; the same tickets can be used on buses and trams, except for airport express buses (€4). Useful routes include Nos 17 and 22 for the Musée Matisse in Cimiez, 38 for the Musée des Beaux-Arts, 9 or 10 for the Parc Floral Phoenix.

Buses in Cannes are run by Bus Azur (www.busazur.com); most pass the rail and bus stations. Monaco has five public bus routes daily; lines 1 and 2 run between the Casino area (boulevard des Moulins) and Monaco-Ville; individual tickets cost €1.

Regional bus services between Nice, Cannes and Menton are run by RCA (Rapides Côte d'Azur, www.rca.tm.fr). Nice's bus station (*gare routière*) is at 5 boulevard Jean Jaurès.

Trains. The TER regional network links the coastal towns, with branch lines inland from Cannes to Grasse and Nice to Cuneo; timetables can be downloaded on www.ter-sncf.com/paca/index.asp. Enquire about various categories of tickets for tourists, children, families, under-26s and OAPs. Eurail passes and Inter-rail cards are valid. See also www.voyages-sncf.fr.

Taxis. Nice: Central Taxi Riviera (tel: 04 93 13 78 78); Nice's taxis are notoriously expensive. Cannes: Allo Taxi Cannes (tel: 08 90 71 22 27, www.taxicannes.fr). Monaco: Monaco Taxi (tel: 08 20 20 98 98).

R

RELIGION

France is a predominantly Roman Catholic country, with minority Protestant, Muslim and Jewish communities. Non-Catholic services are called *cultes* and Protestant churches are known as *temples*. Roman Catholicism is the established religion in Monaco. Nice,

Cannes and Monaco each have English-speaking Protestant services.
Holy Trinity Anglican Church, 11 rue de la Buffa, Nice, tel: 04 93
87 19 83, www.anglican-nice.com
Holy Trinity Anglican Church, 2–4 avenue du Général Ferrie,
Cannes, tel: 04 93 94 54 61, http://holytrinity.free.fr
St Paul's Anglican Church Monaco, 22 avenue de Grande-Bretagne,
Monte Carlo, tel: +377-93 30 71 06

S

SMOKING

Smoking is prohibited in all state-owned buildings, in public places
and on public transport, including restaurants, bars, etc, except in
specially ventilated sealed-off *fumoirs* or outside on café terraces;
smoking is banned in public areas of hotels, but not in hotel bedrooms unless they are designated non-smoking rooms.

T

TELEPHONES

Many public phones only accept *télécartes* (phone cards), which can
be bought at post offices and tobacconists. Specify if you want a
carte à puce (works only in phone boxes) or a *carte à code* (works
from any phone). The latter tend to have better international rates.
A surcharge will be added for calls made from your hotel room.

France uses a 10-digit telephone-number system, whether it is a
local or long-distance call. Numbers on the French Riviera begin
with 04. Mobile phone numbers start with 06; special-rate numbers
start with 08, varying from freephone 0800 to premium rate 0892.

When calling France from abroad, dial the French country code
33 and omit the initial 0. The country code for Monaco, which is
not on the 10-digit system, is 377. When making overseas calls from
France, dial 00 followed by the country code and then the number.

Directory enquiries: various providers, all starting with 118.

Mobile phones. If you are using a British-based mobile in France, dial as if you were a local subscriber. To call from one British phone to another, use the international code even if you are both in France.

TIME ZONES

France and Monaco follow Greenwich Mean Time + 1; between March and October the clocks are put forward one hour.

TIPPING

A 10–15 percent service charge is included in hotel and restaurant bills (to be sure, check for *service compris* on the bill), although rounding up bills with a few coins is appreciated. It is also usual to give hotel porters, filling-station attendants, etc, a few coins, e.g.:

Hotel porter, per bag	€1
Lavatory attendant	€0.50
Taxi driver	round up to nearest €5 (optional)
Tour guide, half-day	€2–4

TOILETS

There are free toilets in museums and department stores. If using a toilet in a café, it is polite to order at least a coffee at the bar.

Where are the toilets?   **Où sont les toilettes?**

TOURIST INFORMATION

Nice: 5 promenade des Anglais, tel: 08 92 70 74 07, www.nice tourisme.com; Mon–Sat 9am–7pm, until 6pm in winter. Branches at Nice train station (avenue Thiers) and Nice airport (T1).

Cannes: Palais des Festivals, La Croisette, tel: 04 92 99 84 22, www.cannes-hotel-booking.com; daily 9am–8pm, until 7pm in winter. Branches at the station and La Bocca.

Monaco: Direction de Tourismes, 2a boulevard des Moulins, Monte Carlo, tel: +377-92 16 61 16, www.visitmonaco.com.

Maison de France (national tourist board) can supply brochures before you go; websites in English on www.franceguide.com.

Australia: Level 13, 25 Bligh Street, Sydney, NSW 2000, tel: 02 9231 5244.

Canada: 1080 Avenue McGill College, Suite 1010, Montréal, Québec H3A 2W9, tel: 514 288 2026.

UK: Lincoln House, 300 High Holborn, London WC1V 7JH, tel: 09068 244123 (premium rate).

US: 825 Third Avenue, 29th floor (entrance on 50th Street), New York, NY 10022, tel: 514 288 1904.

W

WEBSITES AND INTERNET

Wifi is now available in many hotels, which means that the number of internet cafés has declined; there are also hotspots in numerous cafés and at Nice airport.

Useful general websites (see also official sites above):

www.beyond.fr   **www.guideriviera.com**
www.cannes.com   **www.monte-carlo.mc**
www.cote.azur.fr   **www.nicerendezvous.com**
www.culture.fr   **http://riviera.angloinfo.com**

Y

YOUTH HOSTELS *(auberges de jeunesse)*

Nice has two youth hostels affiliated to the Fédération Unie des Auberges de Jeunesse (www.fuaj.org):

Les Camélias, 3 rue Spitalieri, tel: 04 93 62 15 54. In the town centre.

Mont Boron, route Forestière du Mont Alban, tel: 04 93 89 23 64. On a wooded hill 4km (2½ miles) from central Nice.

Recommended Hotels

Nice and Cannes are among the towns with the largest quantity and variety of accommodation in France, ranging from the grandiose seafront 'palace hotels' to small family-run places in converted townhouses. Even so, they can be heavily booked during major events and in the high summer. Monaco's hotels are mainly geared to the luxury end of the market, although there are a few small, inexpensive options in La Condamine. The symbols below indicate the average cost of a double room per night in high season, including TVA (VAT), but generally excluding breakfast. An additional tourist tax is charged per person per night, which varies according to the official star rating. All hotels listed have air conditioning and private bathrooms with bath or shower unless indicated. Many hotels also have triple or family rooms, or can add a bed (sometimes for a fee) for a child. The traditional breakfast of coffee, baguette and croissants is increasingly being replaced by a generous buffet. Prices may be lower in winter, but rocket for special events such as Monaco Grand Prix and Cannes Film Festival. Look out also for special packages and last-minute deals on the internet. All the hotels listed take major credit cards unless otherwise stated.

€€€€€	over €380
€€€€	€260–380
€€€	€160–260
€€	€90–160
€	below €90

NICE

Hi Hôtel €€€–€€€€ *3 avenue des Fleurs, 06000 Nice, tel: 04 97 07 26 26, www.hi-hotel.net.* The hip and colourful Hi Hôtel has become a cult address for design fans, where Matali Crasset's nine different room concepts encourage you to experiment with new ways of living – bath in the middle of the room, pontoon living, high-tech, four-poster bath and operating table bed. There's an organic snack bar and restaurant and DJs in the bar at weekends. The rooftop sundeck has a minuscule pool.

Hôtel Aria €€ *15 avenue Auber, 06000 Nice, tel: 04 93 88 30 69, www.aria-nice.fr.* This good-value, recently renovated 19th-century hotel overlooks an attractive garden square amid the Belle Epoque and Art Deco buildings of the Musicians' Quarter. Rooms are light and high-ceilinged, in sunny colours.

Hôtel Beau Rivage €€€€ *24 rue St-François-de-Paule, 06300 Nice, tel: 04 92 47 82 82, www.nicebeaurivage.com.* Located near the Opéra, the hotel where Matisse stayed when he first came to Nice is now a gorgeous exercise in sophisticated minimalism, decorated in natural wood and tones of grey by architect Jean-Michel Wilmotte. TV and internet in every room. In summer, Les Galets restaurant is replaced by the Beau Rivage beach restaurant.

Hôtel du Petit Palais €€ *17 avenue Emile Bieckert, 06000 Nice, tel: 04 93 62 19 11, www.petitpalaisnice.com.* A small, friendly hotel in the pretty ochre-coloured villa on Cimiez hill that once belonged to actor-playwright Sacha Guitry. Some rooms have small terraces or balconies with views over Nice and the Baie des Anges, and there's a small paved garden courtyard.

Hôtel Ellington €€€–€€€€ *25 boulevard Debouchage, 06000 Nice, tel: 04 92 47 79 79, www.ellington-nice.com.* An elegant town centre hotel, recently redone as a homage to jazz, with an atmospheric 1950s speakeasy-style whiskey bar downstairs and photos of jazz musicians in lifts and corridors. Bedrooms vary between black-and-white minimalism and a more traditional Provençal style.

Hôtel Gounod €€ *3 rue Gounod, 06000 Nice, tel: 04 93 16 42 00, www.gounod-nice.com.* A comfortably refurbished Belle Epoque hotel in the Musicians' Quarter. Guests have access to the pool, spa and gym of the modern but ugly Splendid Hôtel next door.

Hôtel Grimaldi €€–€€€ *15 rue Grimaldi, 06000 Nice, tel: 04 93 16 00 24, www.le-grimaldi.com.* A lovely intimate hotel in the New Town stretching between two Belle Epoque houses on either side of a central courtyard. Helpful staff and comfortable good-sized rooms decorated with colourful neo-Provençal fabrics.

Hôtel Ibis Centre Gare € *14 avenue Thiers, 06000 Nice, tel: 04 93 88 85 55, www.accorhotels.com.* A big, modern branch of the budget chain located near the train station. The 199 rooms offer standard chain decor, but the price is hard to beat, the service efficient and the outdoor swimming pool is a rare plus.

Hôtel La Pérouse €€€–€€€€€ *11 quai Rauba Capéu, 06300 Nice, tel: 04 93 62 34 63, www.hotel-la-perouse.com.* A luxurious secluded hotel with an astonishing location hidden up Castle Hill, reached by lift from the quayside, with stunning views over the Baie des Anges. Comfortable traditional rooms, some with a terrace. Swimming pool and an outdoor restaurant open only in summer. Small fitness room.

Hôtel Negresco €€€€€ *37 promenade des Anglais, 06000 Nice, tel: 04 93 16 64 00, www.hotel-negresco-nice.com.* Under its pink-and-green cupola, the Negresco is both Nice's most celebrated hotel and one of its most eccentric, with a mix of elegance and kitsch. Original Old Master paintings, modern sculptures by Nikki de Saint Phalle and a winter garden by Gustave Eiffel mix with gold-plated basins and curiously tacky souvenir shops, while the rooms are furnished with antiques and satin flourishes. There are two restaurants: the haute-cuisine Chantecler and the merry-go-round-themed La Rotonde. Private beach in front of the hotel.

Hôtel Rex € *3 rue Masséna, 06000 Nice, tel: 04 93 87 87 38, www.hotel-rex.com.* A tiny, tasteful budget hotel. The entrance on a busy street just off place Masséna doesn't look promising, but once upstairs (no lift), the rooms reached via a bridge over the courtyard are clean and pretty, in soft pastel tones. No air con.

Hôtel Suisse €€–€€€ *15 quai Rauba Capéu, 06300 Nice, tel: 04 92 17 39 00, www.hotels-ocre-azur.com.* Behind a period facade virtually built into the cliff face of Castle Hill, the attractive Hôtel Suisse has been stylishly modernised with a different colour scheme on each floor. Most rooms have a sea view and balcony. The gorgeous ground-floor salon includes a tiny cave.

Hôtel Westminster €€€–€€€€ *27 promenade des Anglais, 06000 Nice, tel: 04 92 14 86 86, www.westminster-nice.com.* This venerable pink-stucco seafront hotel has preserved its impressive ground-floor salons and the magnificent open staircase, hung with an interesting collection of historic oil paintings of Vieux Nice. Bedrooms have gradually been redone floor by floor – some in traditional style, the most recent ones in more contemporary soft pearly blues with subtle lighting. Restaurant and bar.

Hôtel Windsor €€–€€€ *11 rue Dalpozzo, 06000 Nice, tel: 04 93 88 59 35, www.hotelwindsornice.com.* From the outside it looks like any 19th-century hotel, but within is a true one-off. Many of the rooms have been individually decorated by internationally renowned contemporary artists, including Robert Barry, Lily van der Stokker, François Morellet, Peter Fend, Jean le Gac, and Ben, who has written all over the walls. Simpler rooms have frescoes or posters. There's a Turkish bath and fitness room, plus outdoor swimming pool and aviary in the lushly planted garden.

Villa La Tour €–€€ *4 rue de la Tour, 06300 Nice, tel: 04 93 80 08 15, www.villa-la-tour.com.* With just 14 rooms in a former monastery, the Villa La Tour is for romantics who want to stay in the Old Town itself. Squashy decrepit sofas in the entrance and individually decorated rooms have a boho charm. You pay slightly more for a view over the Vieux Nice rooftops. No lift.

CANNES

Carlton Intercontinental €€€€€ *58 La Croisette, 06400 Cannes, tel: 04 93 06 40 06, www.intercontinental.com/cannes.* The legendary palace hotel where the jury stays during the film festival has a sweeping Belle Epoque facade and sumptuous suites. It helps to have film-star means as standard rooms can be disappointingly small; avoid those at the rear without sea views. Two restaurants, and private beach, health club and swimming pool.

Hôtel Cavendish €€€–€€€€ *11 boulevard Carnot, 06400 Cannes, tel: 04 97 06 26 00, www.cavendish-cannes.com.* A characterful boutique hotel in an attractive Belle Epoque building on the boulevard that leads towards La Croisette. The comfortable period townhouse style was conceived by decorator Christophe Tollemer as a homage to the English lords who once frequented the coast; some wonderful circular rooms in the corner turret.

Hôtel Château de la Tour €€€ *10 avenue Font-de-Veyre, 06150 Cannes La Bocca, tel: 04 93 90 52 52, www.hotelchateaudelatour. com.* On the hill above the Plage du Midi, this is a rare place where you can capture a taste of the aristocratic villa lifestyle – the original wing complete with crenellated turret was built for a countess in the 1880s. Comfortable traditional rooms. The restaurant, open to non-residents, moves out in summer to the exotically planted garden, where there is also an outdoor pool.

Hôtel Martinez €€€€–€€€€€ *73 La Croisette, 06400 Cannes, tel: 04 92 98 73 00, www.hotel-martinez.com.* The splendid facade, acres of marble hallways and grand staircase perpetuate the Art Deco glamour of the 1920s when it was built by Frank Martinez. The 412 bedrooms alternate between classic and Deco style. Two vast penthouse apartments have huge roof terraces, butler service and Turkish baths. Facilities include the Palme d'Or restaurant, Givenchy spa and the trendy Z'Plage in summer.

Hôtel Molière €€ *5 rue Molière, 06400 Cannes, tel: 04 93 38 16 16, www.hotel-moliere.com.* Small, well-placed contemporary design hotel with colourful minimalist rooms, at the rear of a long flowery garden; most rooms have balconies.

Hôtel Splendid €€€ *4–6 rue Félix Faure, 06400 Cannes, tel: 04 97 06 22 22, www.splendid-hotel-cannes.fr.* A sparkling white Belle Epoque edifice splendidly placed in the heart of the action, near the port and almost opposite the Palais des Festivals. Rooms have been comfortably updated while retaining period flourishes; breakfast is served on a large sunny terrace.

Le Mistral Hôtel €€ *13 rue des Belges, 06400 Cannes, tel: 04 93 39 91 46, www.mistral-hotel.com.* A great budget discovery in a simple blue-shuttered building just a couple of streets back from the Palais des Festivals, with friendly staff and compact but comfortable rooms in colourful minimalist style. No lift.

MONACO

Hôtel de France € *6 rue de la Turbie, La Condamine, 98000 Monaco, tel: +377-93 30 24 64, www.monte-carlo.mc/france.* This friendly budget hotel on a side street has an air of the provinces. Rooms are not air-conditioned but have ceiling fans and are clean and tastefully decorated with colourful fabrics. No lift.

Hôtel de Paris €€€€€ *place du Casino, Monte Carlo, 98000 Monaco, tel: +377-92 16 30 00, www.montecarloresort.com.* The hotel that started it all in 1864 has welcomed anyone who is anyone and is still the grandest place to stay in Monte Carlo, with chandelier-hung lobby, grand staircase and bedrooms and suites that remain firmly in the spirit of another age. Home to the ever-fashionable Bar Américain, the gourmet Louis XV restaurant and with direct access to Les Thermes Marins spa and gym.

Hôtel Hermitage €€€€€ *square Beaumarchais, Monte Carlo, 98000 Monaco, tel: +377-92 16 40 00, www.montecarloresort.com.* This Belle Epoque grande dame queens it over Monte Carlo. Already a giant when it opened in the 1880s, it has gone on adding bits ever since, the latest being two new floors and a rooftop putting green, but the winter garden with stained-glass dome by Gustave Eiffel remains the centrepiece. The best rooms have balconies and sea views. Direct access to Les Thermes Marins spa.

Hôtel Métropole Monte Carlo €€€€€ *4 avenue de la Madone, Monte Carlo, 98000 Monaco, tel: +377-93 15 15 15, www.metropole.com.* Behind an astonishing curtain of vegetation, this grand 1880s hotel has been magnificently refurbished by decorator Jacques Garcia. The 141 bedrooms are plush, with lavish fabrics and mahogany and marble bathrooms. There's a cocktail bar, ESPA spa, seawater pool and the Joël Robuchon restaurant.

Hôtel Miramar €€ *1 avenue Président J-F Kennedy, La Condamine, 98000 Monaco, tel: +377-93 30 86 48, www.hotel-miramar.mc.* A bargain 11-room hotel above a brasserie overlooking the Port Hercule with fine views of the Palais Princier on the other side. Rooms have a vaguely nautical theme in hemp, wood and natural tones; some have balconies. Friendly staff.

Hôtel Olympia €€ *17bis boulevard du Général Leclerc, 06240 Beausoleil, tel: 04 93 78 12 70, www.olympiahotel.fr.* Just across the border into France but only a short walk from the Casino, the Belle Epoque Olympia has been recently renovated. Corner rooms have attractive bow windows.

Hôtel Port Palace €€€€ *7 avenue Président J-F Kennedy, La Condamine, 98000 Monaco, tel: +377-97 97 90 00, www.port palace.com.* All 50 rooms and suites have harbour views at this sleek, modern design hotel by the port. There are luxurious leather and marble finishes and floors themed by sea, shells, rock, sun and air. Gym and spa but no pool. The rooftop restaurant serves Mediterranean cuisine.

Le Méridien Beach Plaza €€€€ *22 avenue Princesse Grace, Monte Carlo, 98000 Monaco, tel: +377-93 30 98 80, www.lemeridien. com.* Just east of Larvotto Beach, the huge, modern Méridien Beach has contemporary artworks in the lobby and a 24-hour restaurant where you can watch the chefs cooking in the circular open kitchen. Landscaped outdoor pool, indoor pool and private beach. Two mirror towers provide a high-tech 180° vision of the sea; many of the other guest rooms have balconies with sea views.

Novotel Monte Carlo €€€ *16 boulevard Princesse Charlotte, Monte Carlo, 98000 Monaco, tel: +377-99 99 83 00, www.novotel. com.* Built on the former site of Radio Monte Carlo, architect Jean-Michel Wilmotte's brand-new building emphasises cream stone, natural wood and glass in a very upmarket branch of the modern business chain. There are 218 spacious, minimalist bedrooms, an outdoor pool, a gym and a restaurant with menu conceived by Jacques Maximin.

THE ESTÉREL

Miramar Beach Hôtel €€€–€€€€ *47 avenue de Miramar, 06590 Théoule-sur-Mer, tel: 04 93 75 05 05, http://mbhriviera. com.* Located west of Cannes at the foot of the Estérel massif. Comfortable rooms, most with sea views, are all done out in Provençal prints. The real pluses are the tropical garden, the steps straight down to the sea and a beachside pool that is covered and heated in winter. There's also a sophisticated Moorish-style spa. The panoramic Etoile des Mers restaurant (**€€€**) does a gourmet take on Provençal cuisine; light lunches are also served by the pool in summer.

MOUGINS

Le Mas Candille €€€€€ *boulevard Clément Rebouffel, 06250 Mougins, tel: 04 92 28 43 43, www.lemascandille.com.* Set in wooded grounds on the edge of Mougins village with views across to the Pré-Alpes, this discreetly luxurious hotel has rooms furnished with antiques in an old Provençal farmhouse and neo-Provençal and neo-Oriental-style rooms in a modern annexe. There's a Shiseido spa, a beautiful outdoor infinity pool and a smaller, sheltered pool for children and families. There's a poolside restaurant in summer and a gourmet restaurant all year round, where Serge Gouloumes combines fine southern ingredients with some unusual uses of spices, plus delicious desserts for the sweet-toothed.

VENCE

Hôtel Diana €€ *79 avenue des Poilus, 06140 Vence, tel: 04 93 58 28 56, www.hotel-diana.fr.* This modern hotel on the edge of Vence's Old Town has been tastefully redecorated after a change of ownership in 2007. Some rooms with kitchenettes. There is a large roof terrace with deckchairs, a Jacuzzi and an exercise machine. A nice place to stay if you're visiting Matisse's Chapelle du Rosaire.

Recommended Restaurants

The restaurants recommended here range from traditional bistros to top gastronomic establishments. Most places serve from around noon to about 2.30pm and from 7.30 or 8pm to around 10pm. Some restaurants only open for dinner during high summer. Brasseries and trendy bar-restaurants may serve food all day. The standard French meal consists of *entrée* (starter), *plat* (main course) and dessert; a cheese course, if taken, is served before dessert. At lunchtime, in particular, it is perfectly acceptable to order just an *entrée* and *plat* or *plat* and *dessert*. Bread is free with the meal, and a jug of table water *(carafe d'eau)* will be served free on request, so it is not necessary to order mineral water. Top restaurants may need reserving several weeks ahead, but it's always worth ringing at the last minute to see if they have a table. At other places, ring a few days before or call before going, especially at weekends and during the high season.

The symbols below indicate the average price of three courses at dinner, without wine, or the most commonly taken set-price menu. Many restaurants also have less expensive menus for weekday lunch. VAT and service, usually 12–15 percent, are included, but service is not always included in Monaco.

€€€€	over €60
€€€	€40–60
€€	€25–40
€	below €25

NICE

Le 26 Restaurant Stéphane Viano €€ *26 boulevard Victor Hugo, 06000 Nice, tel: 04 93 82 48 63.* An elegant modern setting for fresh market cooking. Niçois flavours with more refinement than in the Old Town: try red mullet tart or squid with olives and tomatoes. The lunch menu is one of the best deals in town. Closed Sun.

L'Ane Rouge €€€ *7 quai des Deux Emmanuel, 06300 Nice, tel: 04 93 89 49 63.* The most reputed of the portside venues, where

Michel Devillers serves inventive starters and more classic mains; an emphasis on fish, and surprisingly gutsy flavours. Good, rather formal service. Closed Wed and lunch Thur.

Auberge de Theo €€ *52 avenue Cap de Croix, 06100 Nice, tel: 04 93 81 26 19.* This cheerful Italian trattoria, with an amusing rustic decor of hayracks, farm implements and Neopolitan crib figures, is one of the rare restaurants in Cimiez. Authentic dishes include mixed antipasti, pasta with swordfish, beef tagliata and little babas doused in limoncello. French and Italian wines.

Cave de l'Origine €€ *3 rue Dalpozzo, 06000 Nice, tel: 04 83 50 09 60.* This well-designed wine shop-cum-grocer is one of the new breed of gourmet wine bars and a great place to eat while trying one of the bottles off the shelves. Emphasis on fresh seasonal ingredients, ranging from a plate of multicoloured tomatoes to experimental creations. Closed Sun–Mon and dinner Tue–Wed.

L'Escalinada € *22 rue Paroilière, 06300 Nice, tel: 04 93 62 11 71.* The two whitewashed dining rooms and much-prized terrace are always packed at this Vieux Nice shrine to traditional Niçois specialities, where timeless recipes include sardines *à l'escabeche*, stuffed courgette flowers, gnocchi, ravioli stuffed with *daube*, plus a very good lemon meringue tart. No credit cards.

Grand Café de Turin €€ *5 place Garibaldi, 06300 Nice, tel: 04 93 62 29 52.* This seafood brasserie has been shucking oysters for over a century, drawing a faithful Niçois clientele despite sometimes grouchy service. The speciality is lavish platters of *fruits de mer*, where oysters, crabs and prawns are accompanied by some rarer treats, such as the *violet* (sea potato) and *oursins* (sea urchins) in winter.

Jouni Atelier de Goût €€€€ *La Réserve de Nice, 60 boulevard Franck Pilatte, 06300 Nice, tel: 04 97 08 29 98.* Finnish chef Jouni Tourmanen, formerly of the Louis XV and Ferran Adria, one of the most inventive talents in Nice, has moved recently from his small restaurant in Vieux Nice to this century-old seaside villa west of the port. There's a fashionable bar and a slightly less expensive bistro (€€€ open daily) downstairs. Closed Mon and Sun.

Keisuke Matsushima €€€€ *22ter rue de France, 06000 Nice, tel: 04 93 82 26 06.* Japan meets Provence with brilliant young chef Keisuke Matsushima, who trained with some of France's top chefs. Subtly lit slate tables and geometrical lines provide a suitable setting for his beautifully presented creations – think green, purple and wild asparagus with lemon froth or scallops with truffles, peas and wasabi. There's a good-value lunch menu if you want to sample his style. Closed Mon lunch and Sun.

Kitchen €€ *10 rue Chauvain, 06000 Nice, tel: 04 93 62 88 24.* In a stylish black-and-white interior, with black walls and white panton chairs and oil paintings of 1950s America that bring a touch of a Brooklyn diner, this recently opened restaurant produces modern Med cooking (bruschetta, tuna steak with rataouille, a generous burger) that just happens to be kosher.

Lou Nissart € *1 rue de l'Opéra, 06300 Nice, tel: 04 93 85 34 49.* Between the Old Town and place Masséna, Lou Nissart plays a traditional card with checked tablecloths and a roster of Niçois classics, such as *salade niçoise* and rabbit with herbs.

Luc Salsedo €€€ *14 rue Maccarrani , 06000 Nice, tel: 04 93 82 24 12.* After working at the Louis XV in Monaco and Chèvre d'Or in Eze, among other top restaurants, Salsedo set up on his own with an adventurous contemporary menu that changes every 10 days, in a dressed-up dining room in the New Town. Dinner only July to Aug. Closed Wed, lunch Sat and Thur, and three weeks in Jan.

La Maison de Marie €€ *5 rue Masséna, 06000 Nice, tel: 04 93 82 15 93.* Set back from the street with tables in a quiet courtyard or in an elegant dining room. A stylish take on French and Mediterranean favourites ranges from foie gras, stuffed sardines and herb-encrusted lamb to pasta with scampi. Look for some good Corsican bottles among the Provençal ones on the wine list.

La Petite Nice €€€€ *11 rue St-François-de-Paule; tel: 04 93 85 71 53*. This fashionable hangout of models and celebs located opposite the Opéra is the place to come for elegant versions of local favourites, including *pissaladière*, *salade niçoise* and a *bourride* of John Dory, along with luxury comfort food, such as lobster salad or scrambled eggs with truffles.

Le Safari €€ *1 cours Saleya, 06000 Nice, tel: 04 93 80 18 44*. This market-side brasserie is a Niçois institution, with a great people-watching terrace. Friendly high-speed waiters serve pretty good renditions of local specialities (*salade niçoise*, rabbit, artichoke salad), plus grilled meats and wood-oven-cooked pizzas.

Le Vin sur Vin €€ *18bis rue Biscarra, 06000 Nice, tel: 04 93 92 93 20*. A friendly wine bar off avenue Jean Médecin, popular with young Niçois for its good choice of wines by the glass and accomplished, adventurous cooking. Top marks for a good steak, red mullet with risotto or swordfish with tabouleh and melon juice.

La Zucca Magica €€ *4bis quai Papacino, 06300 Nice, tel: 04 93 56 25 27*. Located on the Vieux Port, the Magic Pumpkin is that rare thing in France: a gourmet vegetarian restaurant that has won over many non-vegetarians. The copious daily no-choice dinner menu wends through a variety of soups, gratins, pasta and stuffed vegetables. Closed Mon and Sun. No credit cards.

CANNES

29 Félix Faure € *29 avenue Félix Faure, 06400 Cannes, tel: 04 93 39 34 93*. This casual brasserie is a useful address near the port as it serves food all afternoon. Wide choice of steaks, generous salads, pasta and pizza.

Astoux et Brun €€ *27 avenue Félix Faure, 06400 Cannes, tel: 04 93 39 21 87, www.astouxbrun.com*. This famous seafood venue behind the port is extremely popular for both its oysters and grandiose shellfish platters and for the people-watching opportunities outside.

Aux Bons Enfants € *80 rue Meynadier, 06400 Cannes, no tele-phone.* In a busy backstreet between the the port and the market, this simple bistro has been in the same family since 1934, serving comforting home-cooked regional food – perhaps grilled sardines and herby Sisteron lamb with courgettes or swiss chard. Closed Sun, plus Sat evening in low season. No credit cards.

Chez Vincent et Nicolas €€ *90 rue Meynadier, 06400 Cannes, tel: 04 93 68 35 39.* At the start of the climb up into the Old Town, this lively new-wave bistro draws a trendy crowd for updated bistro favourites, served against a backdrop of exposed stone, candlelit tables and Cooking TV broadcast while you eat. Service until midnight. Closed some Mondays in low season.

Félix €€€€ *63 La Croisette, 06400 Cannes, tel: 04 93 94 00 61.* Drawing a well-dressed crowd in summer and famous faces during the festival, this luxury brasserie serves fashionable fare in a sleek setting of natural wood and linen with a view of the kitchen.

Mantel €€ *22 rue St-Antoine, Le Suquet, 06400 Cannes, tel: 04 93 39 13 10.* An acclaimed gourmet address in the Old Town, for chef Noël Mantel's elegant southern cooking, such as stuffed vegetables, courgette-flower fritters and fish baked in sea salt. Closed Wed and lunch Thur. Open evenings only in high season.

Le Relais des Semailles €€ *9–11 rue St-Antoine, Le Suquet, 06400 Cannes, tel: 04 93 39 22 32.* White linen and exposed stone walls provide a pretty setting at this upmarket bistro on Le Suquet's main street. The emphasis is on seasonal ingredients from the Forville market. Modern Provençal dishes might include grilled squid in frothy seafood sauce and roast veal with artichokes. Good if pricey wine list. Closed Feb and Sun except during conferences.

Le Restaurant Arménien €€€ *82 La Croisette, 06400 Cannes, tel: 04 93 94 00 58.* Claims to be the only Armenian restaurant on the Côte d'Azur. The cuisine resembles that of Greece, Turkey and Lebanon. Mezze include stuffed vine leaves, hummus, aubergine purée and kebabs. Closed lunch Tue–Sat, plus Mon in low season.

MONACO

Bar Bœuf & Co €€€€ *Sporting Club d'Eté, avenue Princesse Grace, Monte Carlo, 98000 Monaco, tel: +377-98 06 71 71.* Although *bar* (sea bass) and *bœuf* (beef) remain the focus of Alain Ducasse's elegant concept restaurant, new chef Nicolas Lamstaes (who's at the Louis XV the rest of the year when this one is closed) has introduced some other ingredients, such as chicken in a spicy tagine or sea bream. Wonderful service and a gorgeous sea view from the cactus-framed terrace. Closed lunch and mid-September to mid-May.

Beef Bar €€€€ *42 quai Jean-Charles Rey, Fontvieille, 98000 Monaco, tel: +377-97 77 09 29.* A chic modern canteen for carnivores, specialising in different cuts of beef – raw and grilled – from various breeds, imported direct from Argentina, the Netherlands and the USA. There's also a branch on cours Saleya in Nice.

Le Café de la Fontaine € *4 avenue du Général de Gaulle, 06320 La Turbie (just up the mountain from Monaco), tel: 04 93 28 52 79.* Although over the border, this is a great place to eat while staying in Monaco. Bruno Cirino of the acclaimed Hostellerie Jérôme took over the village café and turned it into a relaxed gourmet bistro, serving regional food at remarkable prices. Booking recommended. Closed Mon in winter. Visa and MasterCard only.

Café de Paris €€€ *place du Casino, 98000 Monaco, tel: +377-98 06 76 23, www.montecarloresort.com.* A faithful recreation of the original Belle Epoque bar and brasserie, next to the Casino. Great people-watching on the pavement terrace, plus a restaurant with 1900s decor and slot machines. The crêpe Suzette was invented here, they say. Serves food all day.

Castelroc €€ *place du Palais, Monaco Ville, 98000 Monaco, tel: +377-93 30 36 68.* This institution in Monaco-Ville, with cheerfully frescoed dining room and terrace facing the palace, is the place to try Monaco's Italianate specialities, such as *stocafi* (stockfish). Closed Sat and dinner Mon and Sun.

Joël Robuchon Monte Carlo €€€€ *Hôtel Métropole, 4 avenue de la Madone, Monte Carlo, tel: +377-93 15 15 15.* Joël Robuchon has exported his luxury tapas formula from Paris to Monaco in the hands of emissary Christophe Cusset. Dine on a variety of beautifully prepared, inventive mini dishes, such as foie gras with apricots, artichokes with squid and chorizo and caramelised quail, in an elegant dining room decorated by Jacques Garcia.

Le Louis XV €€€€ *Hôtel de Paris, place du Casino, Monte Carlo, 98000 Monaco, tel: +377-98 06 88 64.* One of the most glamorous restaurants in Europe. Sumptuous decor and immaculate service. The acclaimed cooking by Ducasse, now in the hands of his protégé Franck Cerrutti, takes Mediterranean cooking to the heights of haute cuisine. Advance booking necessary. Closed Tue, Wed except mid-June to mid-Aug, and late Nov to late Dec.

La Note Bleue €€€ *Plage Larvotto, avenue Princesse Grace, 98000 Monaco, tel: +377-93 50 05 02.* This excellent beach restaurant with stylish decor is a relaxed place for lunch under a parasol. Well-prepared, modern Mediterranean-style dishes include plenty of grilled fish. On summer weekends there are free jazz concerts in the evening from quality ensembles. Closed lunch mid-Sept to May, Thur in Nov, and all day in March.

Le Saint-Benoît €€ *10ter avenue de la Costa, Monte Carlo, 98000 Monaco, tel: +377 93 25 02 34.* A longstanding establishment situated in a rooftop position above the Old Port. Classic French cuisine with an emphasis on fish. Closed Mon and Christmas to New Year.

Stars 'n' Bars €€ *6 quai Antoine I, La Condamine, 98000 Monaco, tel: +377-97 97 95 95.* Burgers and Tex-Mex are the name of the game at this hugely popular American restaurant and sports bar, which has racing cars hanging from the ceiling, crash barriers around the bar and drivers' overalls on the tables. There are inside and outdoor tables overlooking the Port Hercule. A friendly welcome for all from small children to racing drivers and pop stars. Service all day. Closed Mon Oct to May.

Le Tip Top € *11 avenue des Spélugues, Monte Carlo, 98000 Monaco, tel: +377-93 50 69 13*. The sort of jovial old-fashioned restaurant and bar that surprisingly does still exist in Monte Carlo feeds steak and matchstick chips, plates of spaghetti and pizzas to local workers at lunch and to absolutely everyone (including, to judge from the photos behind the bar, Formula 1 drivers and Prince Albert) in the dead of night.

EXCURSIONS

CAGNES-SUR-MER

Josy-Jo €€€ *2 rue du Planastel, 06800 Haut-de-Cagnes, tel: 04 93 20 68 76*. In a flowery bohemian setting in an old village house where Modigliani and Soutine once stayed, self-taught chef Josy Bandecchi has made home cooking an art. The speciality is char-grilled meat, followed by Menton lemon mousse or dark chocolate cake. Closed Sat lunch and Sun, and mid-Nov to mid-Dec.

MOUGINS

Alain Llorca Le Moulin de Mougins €€€€ *quartier Notre-Dame-de-Vie, 06250 Mougins, tel: 04 93 75 78 24*. Alain Llorca, previously at the Negresco, took over this legendary restaurant in 2004 and produces some of the most innovative cooking on the Riviera, bringing modern flavours and some influences from his Catalan grandfather, along with fine desserts by his brother Jean-Michel. Set in a gorgeous old olive oil mill outside town; there are also 11 luxurious bedrooms (**€€€€**). Closed Mon in low season.

Le Feu Follet €€ *place du Commandant Lamy, 06250 Mougins Village, tel: 04 93 90 15 78*. A discreetly chic bistro in an old village house. Puts an elegant contemporary spin on bistro cooking.

Le Rendez-Vous de Mougins € *place du Commandant Lamy, 06250 Mougins Village, tel: 04 93 75 87 47*. Amid the cluster of restaurants on the village square, the Rendez-Vous serves simple Provençal food in a convivial atmosphere, 365 days a year.

INDEX

Agay 80

Cagnes-sur-Mer 76–8
Cannes 50–61
 La Californie 58
 Le Cannet 57
 Château de la Tour 56
 Cimetière du Grand
  Jas 56
 La Croisette 51–3
 La Croix des
  Gardes 56
 Eglise Orthodoxe
  Saint-Michel
  Archange 58
 Eglise Saint-
  Georges 58
 Iles de Lérins 58–61
 Marché Forville 54
 Musée Bonnard 57
 Musée de la Castre 55
 Notre-Dame
  d'Espérance 55
 Palais des Festivals 51
 Palm Beach Casino 53
 Plage du Midi 56
 Port Vieux 53–4
 Le Suquet 55
 Villa Domergue 58
 Villa Rothschild 56

Estérel 79–81

Fréjus 81

Monaco 62–75
 Auditorium Rainier
  III 66
 Café de Paris 65
 Casino de Monte
  Carlo 63–5

Cathédrale 71
Chapelle de la
 Miséricorde 70
Chapelle de la
 Visitation 70
Cinéma d'Eté 72
Collection de Voitures
 Anciennes 74
La Condamine 67–9
Eglise Sainte-
 Dévote 68
Fontvieille 73–4
Fort Saint-Antoine 72
Grimaldi Forum 67
Hôtel de Paris 65
Japanese Garden 67
Jardin Animalier 74
Jardin Exotique 75
Larvotto Beach 67
Monaco-Ville 69–72
Moneghetti 75
Monte Carlo 63–7
Musée des Souvenirs
 Napoléoniens 70
Musée des Timbres et
 des Monnaies 74
Musée National des
 Poupées et des
 Automates 66–7
Musée Naval 74
Musée Océano-
 graphique et
 Aquarium 71–2
Nouveau Musée
 National 75
Palais Princier 69–70
Place des Armes 69
Place du Casino 63
Port Hercule 67–8
Princesse Grace rose
 garden 73

Quai des Etats-
 Unis 68
Salle Garnier 64–5
Mougins 78

Nice 25–49
Acropolis 37
Adam and Eve
 house 28
Avenue Jean
 Médecin 41
Avenue Victor
 Hugo 41
'Carré d'Or' 41
Cathédrale
 Orthodoxe Russe
 Saint-Nicolas 44–5
Chapelle de la
 Miséricorde 28
Château de la Tour 42
Château des
 Ollières 42
Cimiez 46–9
Colline du
 Château 31–2
Cours Saleya 27–8
Eglise du Gésu 29
Eglise Franciscain 49
Eglise Jeanne d'Arc 45
Eglise Notre-Dame du
 Port 33
Eglise Sainte-Rita 29
Forum d'Urbanisme et
 d'Architecture 27
Hôtel Negresco 40
Jardin Albert I 35
Musée Archéologique
 47–8
Musée d'Art et
 d'Histoire Palais
 Masséna 39–40

Musée d'Art Moderne et Contemporain 36–7
Musée de Paléontologie Humaine 34
Musée des Arts Asiatiques 44
Musée des Beaux-Arts de Nice 42
Musée International d'Art Naïf Anatole Jakovsky 42–3
Musée Matisse 48
Musée National Marc Chagall 46–7
Muséum d'Histoire Naturelle 37

New Town 37–41
Nice Observatory 47
Opéra de Nice 26
Palais de la Méditerranée 39
Palais Lascaris 29–30
Palazzo Rusca 27
Parc Floral Phoenix 43–4
Place Garibaldi 30
Place Ile de Beauté 33
Place Masséna 34–5
Place Rossetti 28–9
Les Ponchettes 27–8
Promenade des Anglais 38–40

Promenade du Paillon 34–5
Promenades des Arts 35–7
Roman amphitheatre 47
Sainte-Réparate cathedral 29
Théâtre de la Photographie et de l'Image 41
Vieux Nice 25–31
Vieux Port 32–4
Villa Arson 45
Villa Paradiso 47

Saint-Raphaël 80

pocket guide

Nice, Cannes & Monte Carlo

First Edition 2009
Written by Natasha Edwards
Edited by Tom Stainer
Series Editor: Tony Halliday

Photography credits
Mary Evans Picture Library 17; Foodfolio/Alamy 97; Clive Mason/Getty Images 92; Nègre 19; Sylvaine Poitau/Apa 3 top left, 6, 24, 26, 27, 33, 34, 35, 37, 40, 42, 43, 45, 46, 49, 50, 55, 57, 62, 64, 73, 74, 75, 84, 85, 87, 90, 95, 99; Gregory Wrona/Apa 8,10,12, 13, 14, 22, 28, 29, 31, 38, 53, 54, 59, 61, 67, 68, 69, 71, 72, 77, 78, 79, 80, 82, 88, 91, 100, 102, 104

Cover picture: 4Corners Images

Printed in Singapore by Insight Print Services (Pte) Ltd, 38 Joo Koon Road, Singapore 628990. Tel: (65) 6865-1600. Fax: (65) 6861-6438

Berlitz Trademark Reg. U.S. Patent Office and other countries. Marca Registrada

Every effort has been made to provide accurate information in this publication, but changes are inevitable. The publisher cannot be responsible for any resulting loss, inconvenience or injury.

Contact us

At Berlitz we strive to keep our guides as accurate and up to date as possible, but if you find anything that has changed, or if you have any suggestions on ways to improve this guide, then we would be delighted to hear from you.

Berlitz Publishing, PO Box 7910, London SE1 1WE, England.
fax: (44) 20 7403 0290
email: berlitz@apaguide.co.uk
www.berlitzpublishing.com